T0301749

Corporate Philanthropy in China and Beyond

A Comparative Handbook

Series on Dialogue with China

Series Editors: Stephan Rothlin *(Rothlin International Management Ltd,*
Beijing & Hong Kong, Faculty of Business and Law of the
University of St Joseph, Macau, Macau Ricci Institute, Macau)
Dennis P McCann *(Rothlin Ltd, Beijing, China & Rothlin Ltd,*
Hong Kong)

Published:

Vol. 2:   *Corporate Philanthropy in China and Beyond:*
A Comparative Handbook
by Stephan Rothlin and Christoph Stückelberger

Vol. 1:   *Dialogue with China: Opportunities and Risks*
edited by Stephan Rothlin, Dennis McCann and Mike Thompson

Corporate Philanthropy in China and Beyond

A Comparative Handbook

Stephan Rothlin

Rothlin International Management Ltd, Beijing & Hong Kong
Faculty of Business and Law of the University of St Joseph, Macau
Macau Ricci Institute, Macau.

Christoph Stückelberger

Globethics.net Foundation, Switzerland

World Scientific

NEW JERSEY · LONDON · SINGAPORE · BEIJING · SHANGHAI · HONG KONG · TAIPEI · CHENNAI · TOKYO

Published by

World Scientific Publishing Co. Pte. Ltd.

5 Toh Tuck Link, Singapore 596224

USA office: 27 Warren Street, Suite 401-402, Hackensack, NJ 07601

UK office: 57 Shelton Street, Covent Garden, London WC2H 9HE

Library of Congress Cataloging-in-Publication Data

Names: Rothlin, Stephan, 1959– author. | Stückelberger, Christoph, 1951– author.

Title: Corporate philanthropy in China and beyond : a comparative handbook / Stephan Rothlin,
Rothlin International Management Ltd, Beijing & Hong Kong, Faculty of Business and Law of
the University of St Joseph, Macau, Macau Ricci Institute, Macau
Christoph Stückelberger, Globethics.net Foundation, Switzerland.

Description: New Jersey : World Scientific, [2024] | Series: Series on dialogue with China ; vol. 2 |
Includes bibliographical references and index.

Identifiers: LCCN 2023046847 | ISBN 9789811284427 (hardcover) |
ISBN 9789811284434 (ebook) | ISBN 9789811284441 (ebook other)

Subjects: LCSH: Corporations, Chinese--Charitable contributions. |
Corporations--Charitable contributions.

Classification: LCC HG4028.C6 .R684 2024 | DDC 361.7/650951--dc23/eng/20240105

LC record available at https://lccn.loc.gov/2023046847

British Library Cataloguing-in-Publication Data

A catalogue record for this book is available from the British Library.

For any available supplementary material, please visit
https://www.worldscientific.com/worldscibooks/10.1142/13628#t=suppl

Desk Editors: Nimal Koliyat/Pui Yee Lum

Typeset by Stallion Press
Email: enquiries@stallionpress.com

Printed in Singapore

Foreword

China has an unparalleled record of raising some 700 million people out of poverty. But in China as in the rest of the world, there remains an obligation on those who have most benefitted from opening up and reform to aid and enable the less fortunate. The New Era should be marked by those many relatively young philanthropists making a real contribution to poverty alleviation. While philanthropy can never replace the efforts of central authorities, it nevertheless sends a message of prosperous citizens shouldering responsibility for their less prosperous citizens.

Philanthropy takes many forms — supporting education, improving healthcare, and helping local institutions serve better their communities. When too often pursuit of profit is seen as the primary objective, we need to remind ourselves that individual good fortune is only possible when the surrounding society has created favourable economic conditions. Those favourable conditions are created in turn by the efforts of the many.

Building new traditions of philanthropy will strengthen society and help redress the widening gap between rich and poor seen right across the world.

Gordon Brown
Former Prime Minister of UK

Preface

I am delighted to be able to contribute a preface to this handbook for *Corporate Philanthropy in China*. As an entrepreneur, angel investor, and venture capitalist, philanthropy is very important to me and I always strive to place it at the very heart of my business.

I studied biomedical science at university and then completed my Ph.D. in psychiatry. However, I then decided to pursue a career in business rather than medicine. This was above all for one reason — I had concluded that as a successful businessman, I would be able to help more people than I could as a lone doctor. This has remained my vision, my guiding star, in the more than 20 years that have now passed since I founded the Global Group.

If you are already involved in philanthropic activities in China, as I am, you may not see any personal need for a handbook on *Corporate Philanthropy in China*. But my friends at Rothlin Ltd., first, approached me for an interview exploring my experience in the field, especially with regard to the differences between philanthropic culture in Hong Kong and on the mainland. These are considerable and, given the general challenges involved in working in China, they may be enough to convince anyone of the need to "look before you leap," if you hope either to get personally involved in philanthropy in China or to improve your company's performance in this area.

Beyond the very useful and informative sketch of the history of philanthropy in China — which may help explain why the challenge on the mainland is so different from what philanthropists face in Hong Kong, let alone in the West — this handbook highlights a very important lesson:

Success in philanthropy, as in all other aspects of doing business in China, depends on cultivating trust, that is, establishing and maintaining good, honest, and mutually beneficial relationships between donors and recipients.

This handbook tries to be practical about how to develop such trust. It offers a basic review of the new laws governing philanthropic activities and thus clarifies the role that foreign businesses and NGOs may yet play in them. Contrary to what some may believe, these laws, as this handbook shows, respond to real problems that have discouraged the development of philanthropy in China and open a path by which even foreign businesses and NGOs can assist their local partners in meeting standards of transparency and mutual accountability that ought to yield fresh opportunities for ongoing collaboration.

By focusing the spotlight on the challenge of creating and maintaining trust, this handbook gets beyond distracting controversies over keeping score, over which organisations and philanthropic individuals get rankings, or favourable press coverage, or public commendations. It also tries to move us beyond the scandal-mongering, all-too-common in the Chinese (and international) blogosphere, which has created sufficient distrust to retard the development of philanthropy in China and prompted the regulatory reforms we see embodied in the new laws. Such concerns are important, but they mistakenly focus on the needs of donors — and those who would sit on the sidelines criticising them — rather than on identifying and assisting the development of local organisations that may actually make a positive difference in the lives of ordinary people, making a difference to the quality of human life available to our neighbours in need. In the end, this is what philanthropic activities should be all about.

Rothlin Ltd. is to be commended for creating this handbook. It helps everyone in China's philanthropic communities — whatever their level of experience and expertise — to understand the basic challenge of becoming more effective in addressing the needs of our neighbours. And to "love thy neighbour as thyself" — is this not the highest, most concentrated and most meaningful manifestation and expression of our shared humanity and destiny?

Johnny Hon
Executive Chairman,
Global Group International Holdings Limited,
54th Floor, Bank of China Tower, No. 1 Garden Road,
Central, Hong Kong

About the Authors

 **Stephan Rothlin** is Director of the Macau Ricci Institute at the University of St. Joseph, Macau, and Editor of the *Macau Ricci Institute Journal*. His teaching and research interests are focused on international business ethics and responsible entrepreneurship with a focus on China. The Chief Executive Officer of the CSR Consulting firm Rothlin Ltd., Beijing & Hong Kong, he provides educational consulting services to encourage the practice of corporate social responsibility, and advocates, among business communities and society at large, the values of honesty, integrity, respect, transparency, and responsibility as indispensable elements for excellence in business. His publications include: *Teaching International Business Ethics, International Business Ethics. Focus on China* (Chinese version: Beijing, China Social Press, 2022).

 **Christoph Stückelberger** is Professor of Ethics. He has been working on the education of ethics on a global level since the last four decades in various universities: Basel/Switzerland, Beijing/China, Enugu/Nigeria, Moscow/Russia, and Leeds/UK. Over the last four decades, he has worked as head of development and founder, director, and president of three foundations with long-standing experience in philanthropy and new efforts in combining

philanthropy and impact investing. His main field of research and teaching is global ethics applied to economic/business ethics, environmental ethics, trade ethics, finance ethics, political ethics, development ethics, cyber ethics and philanthropy. He is an author and editor of over 70 books and hundreds of articles on applied ethics, all downloadable for free on www.globethics.net/publications. His bibliography is available on www.christophstueckelberger.ch/publishing/. His standard work *Environment and Development: An Ethical Orientation* was published in German, Chinese, Korean, and Indonesian. He is also a consultant on ethics. In 2023, he was appointed as Director of the School for Election Experts in Central Africa (www.christophstueckelberger.ch; www.ethicsconsult.org; www.globethics.net; www.gafoundation.world; www.oikosinvest.org; www.efeac.org).

Acknowledgements

We as authors express our special thanks to the Kingdom Business College, KBC in Beijing for their support for this study! We thank Globethics.net for publishing some of these chapters in its China Christian publication series (www.globethics.net/publications) and the Geneva Agape Foundation for promoting the dialogue and cooperation between European and Chinese philanthropic institutions and persons in training, research, and projects (www.gafoundation.world).

Contents

List of Abbreviations

AVPN	The Asian Venture Philanthropy Network
CCTV	China Central Television
CEPS	Centre for Philanthropy Studies
CFC	China Foundation Center
CNPC	China National Petroleum Corporation
CSRs	Corporate Social Responsibilities
DAFNE	Donors and Foundations Networks in Europe
EFC	European Foundation Centre
EVPA	European Venture Philanthropy Association
GAF	Geneva Agape Foundation
GE	Globethics.net
GDP	Gross Domestic Product
GIIN	Global Impact Investing Network
HNW	High Net-Worth
HNWIs	High Net-Worth Individuals
IPO	Initial Public Offering
MI	Mission Investing
MRI	Mission-Related Investing
NGOs	Non-Governmental Organization
NPC	National People's Congress (China)
NPO	Non-Profit Organization
RMB	Renminbi (Currency of China)
SASAC	State-Owned Assets Supervision and Administration Commission (China)

SMART	Specific, Measurable, Achievable, Realistic, and Time-Bound
SOE	State-Owned Enterprise
SRI	Socially Responsible Investing
SWOT	Strengths, Weaknesses, Opportunities, and Threats
UK	United Kingdom
US	Unites States
WINGS	Worldwide Initiatives for Grantmaker Supports

Introduction

The following chapters[1] provide a guide to the philanthropy landscape and current developments in China, Europe, and Switzerland. It is a comparative study on the overall Chinese and European philanthropy and foundations sectors, their characteristics, and recent development trends within the new global entrepreneurial philanthropy models. We have also given a particular reference to Swiss philanthropy structures. Switzerland is a country with long-standing traditions and a largely developed philanthropy sector.

This handbook is designed as a practical working tool on philanthropic activities and how to get involved with them, especially in China. It aims at helping philanthropists shape their aspirations while guiding foundation managers in their strategic thinking and governance. It should help individuals and organizations find their own answers. The book also includes recommendations on foundations management. There is no single true path to philanthropy and foundations management; it varies by culture and country. Nonetheless, in this guide, we intend to give the readers and practitioners an overall introduction to philanthropy and foundations management.

---

[1] Chapters 5 through 8, with the permission of the publisher Globethics, are based on texts previously published by Globethics, from Jing, Li and Stückelberger, Christoph, *Philanthropy and Foundation Management: A Guide to Philanthropy in Europe and China*. Geneva: Globethics.net, 2017, *China Christian Series 4*. Christoph Stückelberger updated the text, March 2023.

Rothlin Ltd. began its own Corporate Philanthropy Project (CPP) more than 2 years ago before the promulgation of The China Charity Law by the Twelfth National Peoples Congress, effective September 2016, and the related Law on the Management of the Activities of Overseas Non-Governmental Organizations (NGOs) within Mainland China, effective 1 January 2017. Based on original research conducted by Rothlin Ltd.'s staff throughout 2015 and 2016, our initial hope was to investigate three interrelated questions: "(1) How can philanthropic giving by business corporations, both foreign and domestic, achieve the optimum sustainable benefit to Chinese civil society? (2) How can corporations measure and assess the degree to which their philanthropic objectives in China are met? (3) How can a program of corporate philanthropic giving be encouraged and sustained in China?"

The answers we received to these questions, through interviews with representatives of organizations involved in philanthropic activities in China, encouraged us to shift the focus from donors and their concerns towards understanding the needs and capacities of recipient groups. We learned that the key to sustainable corporate philanthropy lies in the quality of the donor–recipient relationships, how these are cultivated and managed, how trust and genuine reciprocity are sustained even through the difficulties that inevitably will arise as their interactions unfold.

Reciprocity is understood in China as *shu* (恕), a nearly untranslatable term that defines the Confucian version of the Golden Rule. When asked by his disciple, Zi Gong, for one word that could guide a person throughout his or her life, Confucius answered: "How about '*shu*' [reciprocity]: never impose on others what you would not choose for yourself?" (*Analects*, XV: 24). The meaning of *shu*, or what the practice of reciprocity entails, can only be learned by observing and participating in basic human relationships, and the shifting patterns of mutual accountability that unfold within them. What one may learn is that human relationships are typically asymmetrical. Sustained over time, they are likely to reverse themselves as, for example, the once totally dependent child grows up and eventually must take responsibility for his or her parents.

Such asymmetry is also evident in the donor–recipient relations characteristic of philanthropy in China. Donors must be prepared to enter into relationships in which recipients learn how to become accountable for the grants they receive, how to become responsible and compliant with the law, and how to mature as genuine partners in philanthropic activities. If donors expect recipients already to have acquired the capacities indispensable for sustaining a genuine partnership, they are not likely to find them. The number of local NGOs in China that are already capable of genuine reciprocity may be fewer than the number of donors eager to work with them. Unless donors are prepared to compete for "worthy" or "qualified" recipients, they are better advised to partner with NGOs that share their sense of purpose and focus on specific areas of concern, and then help them develop appropriate accountability structures as their relationship unfolds.

In subsequent chapters, based on research undertaken by researchers at Globethics, we seek to provide a basis for dialogue between China and Europe, in which mutual learning may be pursued to strengthen philanthropic practice in China. Our chapter on *philanthropy in Europe* adopts an inter-disciplinary approach through quantitative and qualitative data analyses, and countries' case studies, with the objective of giving the readers an overview of philanthropy in Europe. Measurement, characteristics, and trends of the 10 selected European countries have been dealt with from the perspectives of individual giving, and the foundations sector, the fiscal environment, and the new impetus in those countries for European philanthropy have also been discussed.

This is followed by a discussion of the Swiss philanthropic tradition, in which recent initiatives and the legal environment have been particularly addressed. A special characteristic of Swiss philanthropy is the integration of philanthropy with wealth management, linked to the large private industry in Switzerland.

In light of these European comparisons, we take a second look at the *philanthropy and foundations sector in China*. We offer a European perspective on modern Chinese philanthropy, and discuss the factors that affect China's modern philanthropic causes, including its political, economic, and social structures and systems, the regulations and rules of law on start-up funds, and taxability for non-profit organizations. Finally, this study reviews China's new development trends in the philanthropy sector and how the sector is evolving and being put on a broader map, to achieve a meaningful impact.

We finish with a practical guide to *foundations management*, in which the visions, values, and principles for any public benefit foundation are the fundamentals; then, we emphasize the governance and strategic management, and the importance of accountability and financial management. Finally, all foundations, in order to achieve their purposes, need to focus on their action plans, for which they need to first develop their programmes in line with their objectives. Once the programmes are developed, they need to optimally manage those programmes/projects, thus fulfiling their missions and objectives while achieving credibility, recognition as well as outreach. Further, in today's modern communication and multi-media era, for any foundation, it is extremely vital to look into the communication and advocacy area, either through their own website, networks including multi-media, or through organizing events/conferences. These focuses would allow a foundation not only to promote its values and missions, but also to earn respect from the public, thus achieving fund-raising and far-reaching impact.

Stephan Rothlin
Rothlin Ltd.
Christoph Stückelberger
Globethics

Part I

Philanthropy in China: Challenges and Achievements

Chapter 1

The Spirit of Chinese Philanthropy

At the dawn of the 20th century, Dr. Tsu Yu-Yue wrote *The Spirit of Chinese Philanthropy: A Study in Mutual Aid* (1912), summarizing the history of philanthropy in China and sketching its prospects. Before analyzing the three basic categories of philanthropic activity in their historical development, he showed how the spirit of Chinese philanthropy is rooted in the Confucian classics, particularly, the discussions of benevolence and righteousness in the books of Confucius and Mencius. In general, he argues, this spirit was exercised not through the policies of successive Imperial dynasties, but through activities and institutions developed at local levels expressing an impulse towards "solidarity" and "popular democracy." Dr. Tsu expressed the hope that a new national self-consciousness would arise in China in the 20th century, inspiring "a readaptation of the habits of mutual aid and cooperation" (1912: 119).

At the time of Dr. Tsu's writing, China was suffering through the collapse of the Qing Dynasty, brought on by the calamities that had marked the 19th century, a series of rebellions, wars, natural disasters, economic problems, famines, and invasions. China's defeats in the Opium Wars, settled by the so-called Unequal Treaties (1842, 1858), among other things, forced the Qing government to open its markets to foreign exploitation, and its populace to expanded foreign missionary activity. The 19th century missionaries, unlike their 16th century predecessors, typically had little understanding of Chinese culture and traditions, and could only interpret what they witnessed as evidence of Chinese decadence and indifference to the plight of ordinary people. The missionaries responded to their own philanthropic impulses, establishing orphanages, hospitals, schools, and other church-related institutions, all commendable enterprises, of course, but generally informed by the mistaken impression that such had not been part of China's social fabric before their arrival. Dr. Tsu's book was an attempt to correct this mistaken impression. He demonstrated that Chinese philanthropy was the expression of a spirituality deeply rooted in its religious and cultural traditions, and manifest in the creation and maintenance of philanthropic institutions, both public and private, throughout China's history.

As Dr. Tsu indicated, Confucius recognized philanthropy as a virtue, and his disciple, Mencius, believed it was natural to humanity, stemming from the universal and spontaneous disposition of "sympathy" (1912: 17). Wisdom consisted in learning how to exercise this disposition for the sake of those in need of help from others. Mencius described an ideal of "benevolent government," in which a concern for the welfare of his subjects is a fundamental goal for every ruler who aspires to success. As Dr. Tsu points out, there are, of course, dissenting voices in the tradition of Chinese philosophy. He cites at length from the *Zhuangzi*, an imaginary dialogue between Confucius and Lao-tzu, in which Lao-tzu challenges the idea that charity is either natural or beneficial to humanity (1912: 20–23). Though Dr. Tsu rejected Lao-tzu's view as "heretical," clearly the philosophical debate over the nature of philanthropy and its practical consequences has been lively throughout China's long history.

The Spirit of Chinese Philanthropy, however, is not a philosophical treatise but a guide to understanding its institutional development and actual practice in China. Here are some highlights noted by Dr. Tsu:

- The earliest forms of State supported philanthropy in China are "old age pensions" and "poor relief." The establishment of orphanages and other organizations to assist children in poverty are as old as the Zhou Dynasty (1122–255 BCE). Dr. Tsu traces the history of such efforts, especially through the Qing Dynasty.
- While "Poor Laws," mandating "the right to relief of those dependent persons, who may be classed as 'worthy poor'" are of great antiquity in China, the laws typically have been "ineffective," not necessarily because of corruption but because compliance with the laws — and funds to support them — was left to the care of "Provincial and Imperial Administrators" who had more pressing priorities to attend to (1912: 27).

- "Popular Philanthropic Institutions" have tended to flourish in the absence of effective Imperial law enforcement. While such institutions were subject to regulation by the civil authorities, "their support is derived almost entirely from voluntary sources rather than from official ones."
- There are many examples of such "Popular Philanthropic Institutions" that flourished even before the fall of the Qing Dynasty. Dr. Tsu mentions one notable success, "The Hall of Benevolence at Chefoo." Here is his list of the activities sponsored at this institution. It provides us with a benchmark for understanding "charitable activities," as defined in China's new Charities Law: "(1) Non-interest loans to the poor; (2) Burial facilities for the poor; (3) Waste-paper collection; (4) Assisting ship-wrecked persons; (5) Fire protection; (6) Aid to widows; (7) Reception of deserted infants; (8) Free supply of books to the poor who are desirous of reading; (9) Free education for poor children; (10) Orphanage; (11) Industrial school for poor girls; (12) Refuge for the cure of opium-habit; (13) Refuge for the homeless sick; (14) Hospital work; (15) Refuge for the poor in winter; (16) Free kitchen; (17) Vaccination" (1912: 29).
- His own investigation of "Popular Philanthropic Institutions" led Dr. Tsu to lay out three basic categories of Chinese philanthropy, while observing both their common ground and their different focus: "I. Charity, in the strict sense of the word, meaning disinterested aid to the poor; II. Mutual Benefit, or the method of relief and protection by reciprocal efforts; III. Civic Betterment, or the promotion of public welfare through voluntary co-operation on the part of the inhabitants" (1912: 29–30).
- Dr. Tsu summarized the current state of "I. Charity … meaning disinterested aid to the poor": "In regard to relief of the dependent classes, Chinese philanthropy has reached the stage of systematization and institutionality, of adequate relief, but not of scientific prevention of destitution. For instance, charity is ever ready to take in its care deserted infants or foundlings, and spends much energy in bringing them up; but it has not sought to correlate the social phenomenon of infant desertion with other social phenomena, such as fecundity, as cause and effect" (1912: 43). Dr. Tsu thus recognized that popular initiatives that relieve the symptoms of poverty and destitution, however much they may be cherished, will not be enough to address the real

causes, which may require the construction of an entirely different system of political economy on a national scale. A better future for China, in his view, may require unprecedented levels of government intervention.

- Regarding "II. Mutual Benefit, or the method of relief and protection by reciprocal efforts," Dr. Tsu emphasized the moral value of "mutuality" — familiar from the Golden Rule of Confucius summarized in the one word, "reciprocity" or "*shu*" (恕), for example, in *Analects*, XV: 24. Mutual Benefit is embodied in the basic institutions of Chinese civil society, namely, "the clan organization" (1912: 75–83), "the village community (1912: 83–87), and later the formation of provincial and district associations, such as "trade and craft guilds" (1912: 87–90). While "[Mutual Benefit] alone may not be a sufficient agent in the elimination of distress and want … it is a constructive agent because it recognizes the principle of justice, and utilizes the consciousness of social solidarity" (1912: 75).

- Nevertheless, his hope — like that of Confucius' faith in *shu* — is that the principle of Mutual Benefit will expand throughout the nation: "If we conceive of social consciousness within a society as unevenly distributed and concentrating around numerous points that represent the numerous interests and objects to which people associate themselves, and if we conceive of it as ever tending to spread outwards from these points, through friendly social interaction and co-ordination among the different minor social groups and interests until it permeates society generally, then we can think of mutual benefit as at first limited within definite areas such as the clan, the village, the particular trade-guild, and so forth, but as finally overflowing the limitations, and spreading throughout the nation" (1912: 74–75).

- Regarding "III. Civic Betterment, or the promotion of public welfare through voluntary co-operation on the part of the inhabitants," Dr. Tsu describes the apparent paradox of democratic values and institutions emerging from the soil of an Imperial system aptly described as an "absolute monarchy" (1912: 94). Since the District Magistrates appointed by the central government generally lacked the resources required to address the burgeoning needs of their subjects, "the people are left to work out their own salvation in perfect freedom." (1912: 97). Philanthropy as "Civic Betterment" was the peoples' response to the Empire's neglect of public welfare, even before Qing Dynasty collapsed.

- The local institutions of "Civic Betterment" highlighted by Dr. Tsu were voluntary associations focused primarily on providing free educational opportunities (1912: 98–100), public safety and protection (1912: 101–106), free public services such as toll-free bridges and ferries (1912: 107–108), and opportunities for the expansion of municipal self-government (1912: 108–112). Dr. Tsu goes into great detail over the Wuhu Life-Saving Station, which provided "assistance to persons and boats in distress on the river" (1912: 102). His description of the management and finances of the Station, based on the meticulous records kept there, indicate that such associations already had developed capacities — including religious ceremonies — for addressing the challenges of transparency and accountability (1912: 103–105) that inevitably surface when philanthropic organizations grow beyond the traditional networks of family, clan, and village.

Such were the forms of Chinese philanthropy inherited from China's Imperial past. While Dr. Tsu predicts that "with the rise of national self-consciousness and solidarity, philanthropy will acquire a nation-wide basis of operation" (1912: 118), his study enables foreigners who engage in philanthropic activities in China today to recognize the vestiges of these ancient practices still traceable in the local Chinese NGOs with whom they will collaborate. What happened to the spirit of Chinese philanthropy through the vicissitudes of the 20th century is the story to be told in the next chapter.

Chapter 2

Philanthropic Activities in China: Then and Now

2.1 Philanthropy in Post-Imperial China

What happened over the past century, since the collapse of the Qing Dynasty, did not match the hopes that Dr. Tsu Yue Yu had expressed in 1912. The establishment of the Republic of China, and democratic elections to the National Assembly, failed to overcome the forces undermining Tsu's hope for an emergence of a national consciousness. Instead, China had to cope with the resurgence of local warlords, the failure of the Treaty of Versailles ending World War I to reverse the concessions that had been made to the European colonial powers, as well as national disasters like the floods of 1931 in the Yellow, Yangtze, and Huai Rivers. In 1931, the Japanese invaded China in a war of territorial aggression that resulted in the establishment of Manchukuo (Manchuria) as a Japanese puppet state, followed by full-scale military operations against the rest of China that culminated in World War II.

During the initial Republican period (1911–1949), given the chaos resulting from one disaster after another, philanthropy in China came to be dominated by foreign organizations, whose achievements — for example, in the establishment of modern hospitals and health care institutions — while genuine, were vulnerable to criticism as "an icing that deceives and anesthetizes the people" and a "conspiracy to sabotage the People's Republic of China (PRC) by imperialists" (Wang and Zhao, 2014: 20).

The inauguration of the PRC in October 1949 thus involved a dramatic shift away from private — and foreign-dominated — philanthropy towards State supported and regulated social welfare programming. This transformation was accelerated by China's entry into the Korean War in 1950, which involved direct military conflict with the USA and the United Nations forces. By 1954, China established a policy of rejecting even disaster relief from foreign sources, claiming that "the Chinese people can pull through disasters, helping ourselves by engaging in production" (Wang and Zhao, 2014: 21).

- The PRC government's assumption of responsibility for organizing all charitable and philanthropic activities led to the creation of welfare and relief organizations, among the earliest being the Peking Union Medical College (1951), China Association for the Blind (1953), and China Association for the Deaf (1956). Between 1949 and 1954, "666 welfare agencies for the disabled, the elderly, and children were built or reformed" (Wang and Zhao, 2014: 21). During this same period, the Chinese Peoples Relief Association was organized to administer and coordinate among these charities, responsibility for which was eventually transferred to the Ministry of Internal Affairs.
- Social insurance schemes were also instituted, starting in 1951, to address the need for medical and health care services, as well as workers' compensation. The healthcare problems of China's rural population were the focus of the Cooperative Medical System (CMS), "a prepaid collectivized health security system funded by contributions from individual peasant households and brigade (village) and commune (county) welfare funds with additional government subsidy" (Wang and Zhao, 2014: 22).
- "By 1956, there were over 2,100 hospitals at the county level, 20,000 rural medical centers, and 41,000 clinics." These were often staffed by so-called "barefoot doctors — physicians with only a few months training who offered a range of basic medical services" (Wang and Zhao, 2014: 22).
- Thanks to their efforts, "by 1976, 90 percent of administrative villages (production brigades) had adopted the CMS, accounting for over 80 percent of the rural population." The improvement in the health of China's people that they supported is evident from the fact that "from 1952 to 1982 average life expectancy in China rose from 35 to 68 years, while infant mortality fell from 200 to 34 deaths per one thousand live births" (Wang and Zhao, 2014: 22).

The socialist welfare programmes instituted by the PRC government apparently reduced the need for private philanthropy in healthcare, at a time when private resources and foreign aid were virtually nonexistent. Eventually, the government's hopes for the CMS far exceeded the resources invested in it. As the organization of collective farming failed to yield the predicted economic benefits, funding for the CMS dried up, and the programme stagnated. Major upheavals between 1960 and 1975, however, did not provoke a positive reassessment of the need for private philanthropy alongside public welfare programmes. On the contrary, what remained of private charities and the relief agencies that had inherited their mission were subject to intense ideological criticism that led to their dissolution.

- The Red Cross Society of China, for example, which had been reorganized in 1950 under the Ministry of Health, with over 5,000 grassroots organizations, and a half-million members by 1966, was denounced as a "'feudal, capitalistic, and revisionist' force" and "its offices at all levels abolished" (Wang and Zhao, 2014: 23).
- The crisis in social welfare policy is summarized by Wang and Zhou: "Philanthropy was beholden to the political ideology of the time. It was curtailed not only by direct policies, which abrogated the existence of philanthropic organizations, but also indirectly by wider economic and social policy: as economic development foundered in the wake of a series of misguided political campaigns there was a scarcity of social wealth.... Philanthropy had become a river without a source and it would require significant political and economic transformation for this situation to change" (Wang and Zhao, 2014: 23).

But change did come to China, as Hua Guofeng presided over the Third Plenary Session of the 11th CCP Central Committee in 1978, which opened the path towards developing a "socialist market economy with Chinese characteristics:"

- The first of many "government-organized non-governmental organizations" (GONGOs) was founded in 1981, the China Children and Teenagers' Fund (CCTF).
- Soon thereafter came the founding of the Soong Ching Ling Foundation, with Deng Xiaoping as its honorary president.
- While the independence of such GONGOs is debatable, they do mark the re-emergence of philanthropies now regarded as helpful and necessary additions to the State's social security network. Responsibility for

social welfare development was transformed "from being arranged by the state to being held by society" (Wang and Zhao, 2014: 25). After more than thirty years in the shadows, non-governmental philanthropy in China once more was to be encouraged.

In the new era of economic and social reform, two major challenges faced such philanthropic organizations: constructing a regulatory framework that would enable philanthropies to function effectively for the common good and securing adequate funding to carry out their activities. The two challenges, of course, are interrelated:

- "In 1988, the State Council issued its Measures for the Management of Foundations, which defined for the first time the nature and legal status of foundations in China."
- "In 1994, with approval from the government, the China Charity Foundation was legally registered as an independent entity." In 1998 regulations were issued defining the status of such organizations as "people-run non-enterprise units (*minban fei qiye danwei*) and social organizations (*shehui tuanti*)," and framing "the rights and duties, as well as the registration, administration, and supervision processes for these entities" (Wang and Zhao, 2014: 25).
- The potential benefit from such organizations soon became apparent, as later in 1998 serious flooding of the Yangtze, Songhua, and Nen Rivers prompted a mobilization of "all walks of society … to offer financial aid and supplies with donations surpassing seven billion renminbi — the largest donations since the founding of the PRC" (Wang and Zhao, 2014: 25).
- "In 1999, the Public Welfare Donations Law was adopted at the 10th Meeting of the Standing Committee of the Ninth National People's Congress. This law clarified the rights and obligations of donors and recipients, the usage and management of donated properties, and favorable measures such as tax exemption for donors, and also regulated various activities deriving from donations" (Wang and Zhao, 2014: 25–26).
- Between 1978 and 1981, China renewed its participation in the various global health and welfare agencies sponsored by the United Nations, for example, the United Nations International Children's Emergency Fund (UNICEF) and the United Nations Development Program (UNDP). The UN organizations, one by one, set up offices in China

and entered into full cooperative relationships with the PRC government.

- "By the late nineties there are four patterns for philanthropic structures in China: (1) state initiated and managed activities at the national level, (2) state-initiated and managed charity drives and community chest-like foundations at the provincial and local levels, (3) merchant-entrepreneurs and corporate giving, and (4) sporadic independent charity activists" (Zhou and Caccamo, 2013: 4).

The policy shift towards public and private partnerships, both foreign and domestic, thus was accomplished in principle over thirty years ago, establishing the basic context for engaging in philanthropic activities in China in which we operate today.

2.2 Key Concepts: Charity and Philanthropy, Corporate Philanthropy, and Corporate Social Responsibility

Given the complexities of the history of philanthropy in China, it is important to establish the meaning of key concepts defining the discussion of Chinese philanthropy today. The following is meant to map the terrain by providing clear definitions so that we can have a productive discussion of China's new "Charities Law" and the "Law on the Management of the Activities of Overseas NGOs within Mainland China" as these establish the regulatory framework for philanthropies both foreign and domestic. This section will focus on what these and related terms mean for businesses, both foreign MNCs and local enterprises, that expect to do corporate philanthropy in China.

The first task is to understand the distinction and relatedness of two key concepts, namely, charity and philanthropy. The two terms are distinguished in Chinese with *císhàn* (慈善) being the word translating "charity" — with an emphasis on benevolence, compassion, or generosity — and *bóài* (博爱) translating "philanthropy" — with an emphasis on universal fraternity or brotherhood. It is useful to note that the word translated as "Charity" in the new Charity Law is *císhàn* (慈善).

The new Charity Law does not provide an abstract or essential definition of "charity." Instead, it lists a range of legitimate "public interest activities voluntarily carried out by natural persons, legal persons and other organizations through the donation of property, the provision of services or other means":

(1) "Helping the poor and the needy;
(2) Assisting the elderly, orphans, the ill, the disabled, and providing special care;
(3) Alleviating losses incurred by natural disasters, accidents, public health incidents and other emergencies;
(4) Promoting the development of education, science, culture, health, sports and other causes;
(5) Preventing and alleviating pollution and other public hazards, protecting and improving the eco-environment;
(6) Other public interest activities in accordance with this law" (Charity Law, Art. 3).

While these "charitable activities" may be voluntarily carried out by "natural persons, legal persons and other organizations," and thus must "abide by the principles of being lawful, voluntary, honest, and non-profit, and must not violate social morality, or endanger national security or harm societal public interests or the lawful rights and interests of other persons" (Charity Law, Art. 4), the focus of the Law is to regulate "charitable organizations," that is, "legally established non-profit organizations that are in accordance with this law, that aim to carry out charitable activities catering to society" (Charity Law, Art. 8).

The word "philanthropy" does not appear in the translation of the Charity Law. "Charity" therefore may be regarded as inclusive of both charity and philanthropy, since the list of legitimate charitable activities apparently is inclusive of any practices that might be undertaken as an expression of universal brotherhood. The word "philanthropy" may seem foreign, with all too many associations with China's foreign domination prior the 1949. In any event, in China, charity and philanthropy are not usually distinguished.

Charity (*císhàn*: 慈善) is an expression of "the core values of socialism and promote the traditional morals of the Chinese nation" (Charity Law, Art. 5):

- To understand how charity is rooted in traditional Chinese moral values, as well as in the core values of socialism, we need to review the history that informs this term. Though the English word "charity" takes its origins in the traditions of European Christianity acknowledging the idea of love, in China, "charitable activities" are associated less with love and more with basic morality. The relationship linking the two is "benevolence," (*rén*: 仁), whose Chinese character represents a person and the number two. Benevolence is what takes place in an interpersonal relationship. "Fan Chi asked about benevolence. The Master said, 'It is to love humanity'" (樊迟问仁。子曰：爱人) (*Analects* 12.2). The love (*ai*: 爱) that is benevolent (*rén*: 仁) implies active care for others that is expressive of moral righteousness (*yì*: 义).

- Charity based on Confucian virtue thus is not optional, as if it were merely a reflection of personal feeling. It is inherently social, intending social harmony. In Confucian thinking, the distinction between love and justice is blurred. Giving to others in need is a matter of practising basic morality. Charity therefore means becoming socially responsible. Social responsibility is an indispensable quality in human relationships, not only for individual persons but also in the organizations through which they exercise their humanity.

- Distinctively Confucian, however, is the expectation that benevolence is cultivated first in one's own family. The love first learned within the family is best understood as "filial piety" (*xiào*: 孝). Benevolence thus is deeply connected with respect for one's elders and parents, which is reminiscent of the old English proverb, "Charity begins at home."

- Filial piety, however, is much broader than just familial relationships. Filial piety refers to a basic reverence for the origin of life. To be filial is to acknowledge that we do not give life to ourselves but receive it from others. As a general expression of benevolence, filial piety animates all five of the basic relationships (*wǔlún*: 五伦): parent–child, husband–wife, older sibling–younger sibling, older friend–younger friend, and ruler–subject. Each of these constitutes a set of obligations — asymmetrical reciprocities, if you will — that embody basic morality.

- The inherently social nature of "filial piety" (*xiào*: 孝) means that, even if charity begins at home with moral obligations to one's parents and immediate family members, it certainly does not end there. Benevolence and thus charity and social responsibility progressively expand in concentric circles, as one's experience of life moves from internal to external, from *nèi* (内) to *wài* (外). Social harmony, achievable through the cultivation of virtue, is limitless in its expansion. This is clearly the meaning of the Confucian vision of the ideal commonwealth state or

Grand Union (*dàtóng*: 大同), described in *The Record of Rites* (*lǐjì*: 礼记), in *Book IX* on *The Conveyance of Rites* (*Lǐ Yùn*: 礼运).[1]

- As Confucius teaches, when the perfect order prevails, and the world is like a home shared by all, there may be no need for charitable organizations since everyone will carry out their social responsibilities spontaneously and effectively.

- The world as we know it, however, is precariously poised — as in the *Lǐ Yùn* (礼运) — between either a "Small Tranquillity" (*xiǎokāng*: 小康) or an "Infirm State" (*cī guó*: 疵国). The "Small Tranquillity" is a state in which there is sufficient order to ensure that everyone is "well-off" while, by contrast, an "Infirm State" is one characterized by massive corruption and disorder, as well as the sufferings caused by them.

- The social character of Confucian teaching about the virtues thus is clear: virtuous practices, however admirable, are not simply for self-cultivation in any narrowly individualistic sense but are the means to a higher end, namely, the creation of a State in which the people may flourish, by actively participating in the pursuit of the common good.

- The significance of engaging in "charitable activities" thus is clear. They are social obligations rooted in the core values animating Chinese morality. "Charitable organizations" are both possible and necessary because we live in a world struggling to achieve the "small tranquillity" (*xiǎokāng*: 小康) by overcoming the "infirm state" (*cī guó*: 疵国) that lurks in our collective indifference to basic morality.

While social harmony can only be approximated in a *xiǎokāng*, its achievement also requires a State in which laws (*fǎzhì*: 法治) are decreed and enforced for the sake of the common good. Even if charity (*císhàn*: 慈善) is inherent in the traditions of Chinese morality, an understanding of how charity contributes to social harmony — under present circumstances, teetering between *xiǎokāng* and *cī guó* — requires a study of China's laws and the challenges they are meant to address.

Understanding corporate philanthropy and corporate social responsibility in China:

---

[1] "When the great way prevails, the world is equally shared by all" (大道之行也, 天下为公).

- Corporate philanthropy, in the Chinese context, refers to charitable activities sponsored or supported by either foreign or domestic businesses. While foreign businesses, based on their philanthropic experience at home, may approve and sponsor such activities only insofar as they serve a legitimate business purpose — for example, they claim to promote "goodwill" in areas where the firms are seeking to do business by addressing social problems — when doing corporate philanthropy in China, they must be careful to state their rationale in terms that are generally acknowledged there.
- Contributing to China's "social harmony," of course, is a good way to define the purpose of corporate philanthropy, but firms doing business in China must also make sure that the charitable activities they are supporting in fact are consistent with the laws under which they are regulated, as we shall see further on. Some programmes that in other countries might qualify as charitable activities or legitimate examples of exercising corporate social responsibility (CSR) may not be so regarded in China. For example, sponsoring programmes seeking to promote the development of democratic institutions, even at the local level, may not be compatible with the State's current policies regarding "national security" or "societal public interests." The bottom line is that exercising CSR in China in practice means engaging in approved charitable activities. Pundits and bloggers who write on corporate philanthropy in China in the blogosphere may regard generous support for "charitable activities" as something owed to the Chinese people by those who profit by doing business here. They may feel alienated by philanthropic rationales that stress the donors' love for the Chinese people, which they may regard as a mask for covering greed and exploitation. As we shall see in the following section, overcoming such suspicions may require foreigners as well as wealthy Chinese to discharge a formidable burden of proof to demonstrate the sincerity of their commitment to charity.

2.3 The Challenge of Doing Philanthropy in China

During the current era of economic and social reform, corporate philanthropy has grown dramatically. It has also exhibited many "growing pains" that are symptomatic of the historic obstacles to its development, and the challenges yet to be fully overcome.

The dramatic growth is best symbolized by the unprecedented response that Chinese people made to the Wenchuan earthquake (12 May 2008), one of the largest earthquakes ever recorded, in which over 90,000 people were killed, and at least 5 million were left homeless. For a number of reasons, including the Chinese government's openness about the disaster and encouragement of support from all sectors, the philanthropic response was unprecedented: foreign governments and private organizations reported a total of US$456.9 million in cash contributions, and the Ministry of Civil Affairs reported that Chinese public contributed US$1.5 billion, with nearly half of that donated or pledged in the first week.

In addition to the dramatic spike in donations, the Wenchuan earthquake prompted a massive and largely spontaneous mobilization of Chinese volunteers. "The *China Youth Daily* estimated that 200,000 citizen volunteers from all over China descended on the earthquake zone. Beef was trucked in from Inner Mongolia; sleeping bags were brought in from Shenzhen; building material came from Chongqing. Millions of bottles of water and packets of noodles came in from all over.... Many watched television news to decide what to bring. Others learned from early visits what was needed and made repeated return visits. Things like vegetables, which were in short supply in nearby cities like Chengdu, had to be brought in from cities further away from the quake zone. In all $11 billion was given to quake relief" (Facts and Details, 2013). One thing enabling this tremendous response was that for the first time, credit unions and microcredit firms could collect contributions alongside the GONGOs and the government agencies. Observers hoped that the earthquake would mark the birth of a new civil society, ready and willing to support charitable activities for those in need.

Nevertheless, the growing pains accompanying this dramatic increase in philanthropic assistance soon surfaced, in the wake of the Wenchuan earthquake. Even during the initial response, businesses that did not contribute were denounced as "iron roosters" — as if they were as stingy as birds that can't even shed a feather — and then shamed into making substantial contributions. It was clear that even in the new civil society, resentments lingered over the greed and indifference popularly assumed to be typical of business corporations. Later, in the wake of certain problems accompanying the earthquake relief, the Chinese blogosphere began focusing on scandals arising from the alleged failure of celebrities and other Chinese philanthropists to honour their pledges of donations.

The highly regarded Chinese actress, Zhang Ziyi, for example, was severely criticized because of the shortfall between her pledged contribution and the funds eventually delivered by her foundation. After making good on all her pledges, Ms. Zhang conceded that "I wanted to do something good, but we had our problems, such as my lack of experience, my failure to disclose to the public, my limited knowledge about philanthropy and other reasons.... It was certainly a setback. But I learned something new from it." (*China Daily*, 16 March 2016).

Despite her chastened reassurances, Ms. Zhang became a symbol of "celebrity philanthropy," a new term of abuse that critics reserve for celebrities whom they believe — rightly or wrongly — are lacking in sincerity and using token efforts at disaster relief only to restore their fading reputations or advance other personal interests.

If private philanthropies, like Ms. Zhang's foundation, were subject to intense and often excessive criticism, even more so were GONGOs — like the Red Cross Society of China (RCSC) — which was dragged into a scandal involving Guo Meimei, a young adventuress who posted pictures on the Internet displaying her lavish lifestyle while claiming to be a manager at the Red Cross. After the initial furore had subsided, it became clear that the RCSC had experienced a drop in private donations of approximately 60%, even though Ms. Guo later admitted to having no connection with the organization. Nevertheless, as the *China Daily*'s "Weibo buzz" observed, "Due to the Red Cross's long-established shady operation and lack of internal transparency, as well as its already plummeted public credibility following previous scandals, the collective outburst of public doubt triggered by this incident hardly came as a surprise." (*China Daily*, 15 July 2011).

The Guo Meimei incident, itself without foundation, was the match that set off a tinderbox of negative reactions not only against the RCSC but also against most government-sponsored philanthropies in China. As time went on, the heroic stories of solidarity in the aftermath of the Wenchuan earthquake had given way to an increasingly bitter litany of scandals over promised donations either never materializing or, when they were made, often being diverted for other purposes by the agencies collecting them.

In the cascade of allegations regarding waste, fraud, and the mishandling of donations, Chinese philanthropies, both public and private, were facing a full-blown crisis of trust and legitimacy. Here are some significant indications:

- **Yu Jianrong, a professor at the Chinese Academy of Social Sciences observed:** "The incident has triggered a collective outburst of long-time frustration about the Red Cross's murky bureaucracy and questionable governance. And faced with this crisis of trust, the Red Cross Society of China failed to give a reasonable explanation. It will lose its credibility completely if it does not learn lessons from the corruption scandals involving the overspending on meals and other spending irregularities."
- **Wang Ming, the director of the NGO research centre at Tsinghua University, underscored the new demands for transparency and accountability, made possible by the adoption of new technologies, particularly the Internet:** "We're now facing a new world with new technology, where under-the-table transactions are impossible to keep, charity organizations need to have a sense of crisis, to reform in an open and transparent environment where the public will question the credibility of these organizations all the time."
- **In retrospect — as Hu Xingdou, economics professor at Beijing Institute of Technology, pointed out — the government-centred system of charitable organizations appeared unprepared to address these new expectations:** "Most charity organizations in China are monopolized by the state and the lack of any responsibility mechanisms within these charity foundations means their managers can do anything with the donations. Not only does our government not formulate relevant law on charitable funds, but also they never force the charity organizations to make public their accounts, which provide the leaders opportunity to carry out corruption. While the Red Cross must clearly open to the public where the donation goes to, our government should reform the charity system."
- **The need for reform is clear from the comments of microbloggers, like Liu Chun, who defended his colleagues even after Ms. Guo's mischief had been exposed:** "We are not aiming at Guo Meimei, but those commercial organizations behind her that make exorbitant profits out of charity, as well as those charity institutions and activities that lack transparency and regulation. It is high time they stood out to clarify the facts and make public the accounts; it is about time we cleaned up the mess, regulated the procedure and established a transparent, fair and green charity mechanism."
- **Yu Shendu, another microblogger, summarized the nature of the crisis and its possible resolution based on traditional Chinese**

moral values: "Transparency is derived from openness, prestige is rooted in probity."

Of course, in the years since, the government opened the process of legislative reform that resulted in the new Charity Law of 2016. As we shall see, most of its provisions are a response to such calls for transparency and accountability.

Another hopeful sign is that responses to the Ya'an earthquake, once again in Sichuan Province (20 April 2013), show that already much had been done to ensure that the problems in Chinese philanthropies exposed by the Wenchuan earthquake would not be repeated.

Among these hopeful signs was the work of the One Foundation, a properly registered Chinese philanthropy organized by celebrity Jet Li, which by 2015 had donated more than RMB 150 million for disaster relief and reconstruction in Lushan County. One Foundation has been praised for showing leadership among private philanthropies in meeting the public's expectations for transparency and accountability.

- The public's expectations have also led to the development of online charity platforms, like Sina Micro-charities, launched a few months prior to the Ya'an earthquake. In just two days after the earthquake, Sina claimed to have gathered nearly RMB 80.4 million from more than 60,000 Internet users. Similar platforms have been organized through the Tencent Foundation using Alipay, with similar dramatic success. Online charity platforms or "micro-charities" provide the Chinese public with alternatives to the Red Cross and the other government-sponsored agencies previously criticized.
- According to Wang Zhenyao, president of Beijing Normal University's One Foundation Philanthropy Research Institute, increased transparency is evident as such platforms "offer information in a way that allows donors to know where their money is going": "The purpose of each micro-charity project is clear and highly targeted, and the project timelines track how the funds are utilized," Wang said. "This reassures people and makes them want to donate."
- Deng said that charity funds prefer micro-charities to other traditional means because charity projects spend less on promotions online than on TV or in newspapers. The platform also eliminates the inconvenience for donors of travelling to a bank and waiting in line to write a check. "The whole process takes a couple of clicks and the time taken

is almost zero," Deng said. "That makes micro-charities attractive." (*Global Times*, 22 April 2013).

Mapping the terrain of charitable organizations, their potential for transparency and effective delivery of assistance to those in need, has become increasingly complex, here as elsewhere in the world. Though the obstacles to development may be formidable, the potential for significant progress in finding new solutions to perennial problems must also be appreciated. The new Charity Law and its companion, Law on the Management of the Activities of Overseas NGOs within Mainland China, must be welcomed as the government's latest effort to promote such development.

Part II

Chinese Law and Compliance for Charities and Other Philanthropic Institutions

Chapter 3

China's Laws Governing Philanthropy

3.1 The *Handbook of Charity Law of the People's Republic of China* (16 March 2016)

The *Handbook of Charity Law of the People's Republic of China* consists of twelve chapters that comprehensively lay out the new Charity Law — a regulatory framework designed to encourage the development of Chinese philanthropic organizations while also creating conditions of trust, for the government as well as the public at large, through uniform standards of transparency and accountability.[1] As Art. 1 indicates, the Charity Law "is designed to develop charitable causes, promote the culture of charity and standardize charitable activities, as well as to protect the rights and interests of charitable organizations, donors, volunteers, beneficiaries and others who work in the field of charity, while promoting social progress and distributing the fruits of social development." A study of the details of the Law suggests that it achieves its purpose, and impressively so.

As mentioned earlier, the Charity Law defines those individuals and groups to whom the Law applies (Art. 2), the six categories of "charitable activities" (Art. 3), and the principles — they must be "lawful, voluntary, honest, and nonprofit, and must not violate social morality, or endanger national security or harm societal public interests or the lawful rights and interests of other persons" (Art. 4) — that determine genuinely charitable

---

[1] The Handbook is published online by the United Nations Development Program (UNDP): https://www.undp.org/sites/g/files/zskgke326/files/migration/cn/UNDP-CH-Handbook-of-Charity-Law-of-the-Peoples-Republic-of-China.pdf.

activities consistent with "the core values of socialism and promote the traditional morals of the Chinese nation" (Art. 5). The departments of Civil Affairs, nationally under the State Council, as well as provincially and locally, are responsible for administering the Law governing charitable activities.

Since such activities are usually carried out by "charitable organizations," the Law's second chapter defines the seven requirements that such organizations must meet to qualify for legal registration (Art. 9) — among other things, their purpose must be to carry out charitable activities, on a not-for-profit basis, and they must have access to "necessary financial assets" for doing so — as well as the procedures for registering such organizations with the appropriate department(s) of Civil Affairs (Art. 10), including the provision of a "charter" (Art. 11) spelling out a "sound internal governance structure" and book-keeping procedures consistent with "the unified national accounting system" (Art. 12). Charitable organizations, as stipulated in Art. 13, "shall annually submit an annual work report and financial reports to the Civil Affairs departments that they registered with, which will include annual fundraising activities, donations received, management and usage of charitable assets, details of the implementation of charitable projects, and the salary and benefits of the staff of the charitable organizations." Clearly, these measures are meant to ensure transparency and accountability, at least between the organizations and the departments of Civil Affairs that must regulate them.

Further provisions in the Charity Law's second chapter cover potential conflicts of interest involving "the founders, major donors and management staff" when engaged in any business transaction with the organization (Art. 14), as well as a prohibition against any activities that would endanger "national security and societal public interests," or create any other legal problems for donors or beneficiaries (Art. 15). Similarly, Art. 16 stipulates the conditions that would disqualify a person from serving as "the leader of a charitable organization." The second chapter, then, closes out with the criteria for terminating a charitable organization (Art. 17), and the procedures for "liquidating" such organizations and disposing of their remaining assets (Art. 18).

Fund-raising is the focus of the third chapter of the Charity Law. There are two kinds of fund-raising, "public" and "targeted" (Art. 21), the difference being that "public" fund-raising appeals are "directed at society at large," while "targeted" efforts are "directed at specific targets," that is, specific prospective donors. There are, of course, licenses that must be obtained to engage legally in either kind of charitable fund-raising. Article 22 stipulates how such fund-raising "certificates" can be obtained through the relevant departments of Civil Affairs, while Art. 23 mandates the kinds of methods permitted for public fund-raising, including using internet platforms designed and registered for that purpose. Articles 28 through 31 make similar provisions for "targeted" fund-raising activities, and the chapter finishes by clarifying the boundaries for both kinds of fund-raising, including standard prohibitions against coercive or fraudulent methods. Here, as in other areas, the Charity Law seeks to enforce basic standards of good business ethics.

The fourth chapter of the Charity Law stipulates the nature of legitimate charitable donations, instructs donors and beneficiaries on how to make them, and stipulates reasonable procedures for protecting donors and beneficiaries, including the issuing of receipts (Art. 38), written donation agreements (Art. 39), and the obligation of donors to fulfill their pledges (Art. 41). One very specific area covered here is a prohibition against commercial schemes masked as charitable fund-raising, for the promotion of certain items, like tobacco and other products "prohibited from being publicized by laws" (Art. 40).

The Charity Law's fifth chapter defines "charitable trusts" and stipulates the procedures for establishing these. Since the "principals" or "trustees" that administer such trusts have "fiduciary duties" (Art. 47) that may not be breached, the chapter details procedures to ensure their proper management, including the provision of "trust supervisors [who] monitor the actions of trustees, and safeguard the interests of principals and beneficiaries in accordance with the law" (Art. 49). Here again, the Charity Law clearly is designed to promote transparency and accountability in accordance with basic principles of good business ethics supported by an effective regulatory framework.

The sixth chapter addresses the "financial assets of a charitable organization" and their proper management. Such assets "can only be used for charitable purposes in accordance with the organizational charter and the donation agreement and must not be distributed among the founders, donors or members of the organization" (Art. 52). Embezzlement of funds or other misappropriations are expressly prohibited, and provisions are established for reports designed to minimize the risk of such abuses. At the same time, the law stipulates the conditions for investing these financial assets to increase their value, consistent with previous directives from the civil department of the State Council (Art. 54). Such investment strategies do not undermine a charitable organization's status as a not-for-profit institution. The chapter concludes with a series of regulations governing the use and disposal of any properties donated to charitable organizations. It makes explicit certain ceilings on annual expenditures for fund-raising and management fees (Art. 60) to ensure that charitable organizations carry out their missions efficiently and fairly.

The purchase of "Charitable Services" is regulated in the seventh chapter (Arts. 61–68), including the recruitment and management of "volunteers." The law specifically emphasises the need to respect the human dignity and privacy of beneficiaries (Art. 62), especially in the provision of "medical rehabilitation and educational training" services.

The eighth chapter regulates "Disclosure of Information" in all aspects of a charitable organization's performance. It stipulates the kinds of "charity information" to be collected and published regularly by the relevant departments of Civil Affairs (Art. 70) and provides other regulations designed to ensure, on the one hand, timely disclosure, while also, on the other hand, respecting proper limits on such disclosures: "Information regarding state secrets, individual privacy, commercial secrets, as well as information such as the names, titles, addresses and contact methods of donors and principals of charitable trustees who do not consent to it being disclosed, must not be disclosed." (Art. 76).

The "Promotional Measures" outlined in Chapter 9 (Arts. 77–91) stipulate the ways in which the "relevant departments of the people's governments" will develop programmes to assist the development of charitable organizations, including sufficient publicity regarding their registration procedures. The promotional measures include tax benefits for donors — organizations as well as individuals — as well as beneficiaries of charitable activities (Arts. 79–81). The chapter also notes that "overseas donations towards charitable activities are eligible for a reduction or exemption from import duties and import value-added tax in accordance with the law" (Art. 80). It also encourages schools and educational institutions, radio broadcasters, television stations, newspapers, the internet, and other media to "adopt measures to promote a culture of charity and cultivate citizens' awareness of charity" (Art. 88).

Chapters 10 and 11 detail regulations for the government agencies, especially Civil Affairs departments, performing their responsibilities for supervising and managing charitable organizations. Chapter 10 stipulates how investigations of charitable organizations are to be conducted (Arts. 93–94), and the procedures to be followed when such organizations are discovered breaking the law (Art. 97). Chapter 11, on "Legal Responsibility" (Arts. 98–107), describes the penalties and sanctions that may be levied against such violations of the law. The final articles (Arts. 108–109) in this chapter, however, stipulate the penalties that the relevant government agencies may face if they abuse their powers in performing their responsibilities. Article 108 is explicit in identifying six specific areas that will trigger "disciplinary action."

The new Charity Law should create a very positive impression for all concerned. It is comprehensive, reasonable, and genuinely committed to the development of charitable organizations among the people of China and for the people of China. While it is not focused on the concerns of foreign donors and foreign charitable organizations operating in China — concerns that are addressed, at least partially, in the new "Law on the Management of the Activities of Overseas NGOs within Mainland China" outlined in the next section — it clearly establishes ways for foreigners to participate in charitable activities in China, by acknowledging possible tax exemptions (Art. 80) and establishing a regulatory framework that encourages the development of transparent and accountable "charitable organizations" capable of meeting the expectations of international donors and institutions.

The new Charity Law, however, appears designed to address Chinese criticisms of public and private charitable activities and organizations that had surfaced, as we saw in the previous chapter, in the wake of the 2008 Wenchuan earthquake. If Chinese charitable organizations make a good faith effort to comply with the stipulations of the new Charity Law, not only will their reputations be improved locally — and, hopefully, their success in attracting local donors — but they will also be more likely to establish themselves as suitable partners for international donors and institutions seeking to participate in China's great work of philanthropy for the sake of economic and social development.

3.2 "Law on the Management of the Activities of Overseas NGOs within Mainland China" (28 April 2016)

As we have seen, overseas non-governmental organizations (NGOs) have played a significant role in the development of corporate philanthropy in China. Therefore, in addition to the new Charity Law outlined in the previous section, we must review the "Law on the Management of the Activities of Overseas NGOs within Mainland China," (the Law or the Oversees NGO Law) promulgated by the Standing Committee of the National People's Congress, on 28 April 2016. The Law came into effect on 1 January 2017.

It consists of seven chapters, ranging from "General Principles" to "Supplementary Provisions." Each one must be well understood if the law is to be implemented properly and complied with carefully, especially by organizations seeking to engage in charitable activities in China.

The major contrast with the Charity Law is that overseas NGOs are to be regulated by the Ministry of Public Security (MPS), rather than the Ministry of Civil Affairs (MCA), which regulates the activities of local charitable organizations. Indeed, the Overseas NGO Law is part of a package of new laws promulgated in 2015 and 2016, intended to build a socialist rule of law in China, including the Counterterrorism Law, National Security Law, the Overseas NGO Law, and most recently the Cybersecurity Law.

The Overseas NGO Law is the first comprehensive regulation of its kind covering all overseas NGO activities in China. Foreign NGOs and their stakeholders, who are subject to the provisions of this law, should resist the idea that a crackdown is imminent against them, fearing that they will be forced to cease activities in China. Though the law may strike some observers as "draconian," we believe its claim to secure a socialist rule of law should be taken seriously, as a basis for forming new levels of transparency, accountability, mutual trust, and cooperation.

Chapter 1 on "General Principles" makes explicit the purpose of the law and defines the organizations that are subject to it. The law is "designed to standardize and guide all activities carried out by overseas NGOs within China, and protect their rights and interests, while promoting communication and cooperation" (Art. 1). It defines "overseas NGOs" as "nonprofit, nongovernmental social organizations such as foundations, social groups and think tanks that have been lawfully established outside of mainland China" (Art. 2). Such organizations that submit to governmental regulation and monitoring, that "work in fields such as the economy, education, science and technology, culture, health, sports, environmental protection, and in areas such as poverty alleviation and disaster relief may carry out activities that legally aid the development of public welfare in accordance with this law (Art. 3).

Operating legally means that overseas NGOs "shall operate according to Chinese laws; not threaten China's security or national and ethnic unity; and not harm China's national interests, societal public interests, and the legal rights of citizens, legal persons, and other groups." Specifically prohibited are engaging in or funding "for-profit or political activities" as well as conducting or funding "religious activities" (Art. 5). Compliance will be achieved through the relevant "Professional Supervisory Units (业务主管单位)" (Art. 6), which will "establish mechanisms to manage overseas NGOs and be responsible for researching, coordinating, and resolving significant problems" emerging from their activities (Art. 7). Those overseas NGOs that comply with the law are promised "the protection of the law" (Art. 4); those that make "outstanding contributions to development of Chinese public welfare" will be commended (Art. 8).

The most important first step for compliance is the process of "Registration and Filing" outlined in Chapter 2. Two options are indicated there, first, registering legally and establishing a representative office, and second, if maintaining a representative office is not possible, filing a "record" of "temporary activities" (Art. 9). Failure to do either is prohibited and will be severely punished.

There are five conditions that must be met for an overseas NGO to register and establish a representative office (Art. 10); but even before they apply they must receive the consent of a "Professional Supervisory Unit (PSU) (业务主管单位)" (Art. 6), which examines and approves the application before it is submitted. While lists of appropriate PSUs will be issued by the relevant public security departments, it remains the NGO's responsibility to obtain PSU approval before submitting its application for legal registration. The documents required for a registration permit are noted in Art. 12. Once approved, the registration will be announced with a certification conveying the registration information listed in Art. 13. The certification will allow the NGO to operate in China legally, get registered for taxation, and establish bank accounts for conducting business. Further articles (Arts. 14 and 15) stipulate the ways to report changes in registration or to legally terminate activities.

Article 16 stipulates how an NGO that conducts "temporary activities" can be approved and certified. The key is to "cooperate with Chinese state authorities, mass organizations, public institutions, and social organizations (hereafter referred to as the Chinese partner organizations, or 中方合作单位)." The documentation required of both the NGO and its "Chinese partner organization" (CPO) is listed in Art. 17. "Temporary activities" are defined as those lasting no more than one year. Any changes must be registered through additional filings. The only exceptions are NGO responses to "emergencies such as disaster relief."

Chapter 3, on the "Regulation of Activities," defines the role of the NGO's representative office, and its responsibilities for submitting and adhering to an annual "activity plan" that must be submitted first to its PSU, and once approved, then filed with the relevant registration management authorities (Art. 19). Regulation includes strict supervision of funding for the NGOs activities in China (Arts. 21 and 22) to ensure that an NGO's activities are consistent with its activity plan. Further provisions regulate tax registration and declarations (Art. 26), recruitment of Chinese staff (Arts. 27 and 28), and the qualifications of the NGO's "chief representative" (Art. 29). Regulation of "temporary activities" is stipulated in Art. 30. Both forms of registered NGOs — those with representative offices and those who partner with approved CPOs to conduct temporary activities — must file an "annual work report" and submit it to the PSU, and then, once approved, have it filed with the registration management authorities (Art. 31). It is strictly prohibited for the Chinese to accept employment or other financial support from NGOs that have failed to obtain proper registration (Art. 32).

Chapter 4, "Favorable Policies," outlines the support that overseas NGOs can expect from the Ministry of Public Security (MPS) and related agencies that will supervise their activities. Among the items mentioned is the publication of a list of approved areas of work and projects and a list of the PSUs to which the NGOs may apply for assistance (Art. 34). Policy advice from the relevant government departments as well as the development of "unified websites to make public the process of overseas NGOs applying for representative offices or temporary work permits" (Art. 35), as well as "tax benefits and other favorable policies" (Art. 36), are promised. Specifically prohibited is the practice of government agencies charging fees "for the annual inspection of overseas NGOs' representative offices" (Art. 37).

Chapter 5, "Supervision and Management," continues the government's good faith effort to demonstrate reform and eliminate corruption by spelling out the rules by which PSUs and government agencies will process the NGO applications and annual reports, investigate illegal activities (Art. 41), and monitor their financial affairs (Arts. 42–44).

Chapter 6, "Legal Responsibility," describes the circumstances under which NGOs will be judged to have engaged in illegal activities (Art. 45), and the penalties to be imposed once they are convicted of these.

Article 46 stipulates the penalties for procedural violations, while Art. 47 enumerates substantive violations liable to judgment as criminal offenses, including subversive political activities and support for religious activities. The penalties range from temporary or permanent suspension of the NGO registration, confiscation of their assets, and deportation of their foreign representatives (Arts. 48–50). By the same token, Arts. 51 and 52 provide general sanctions against any violations of public security regulations by government agents charged with regulating overseas NGOs, including the threat of "criminal charges ... brought in accordance with the law."

A final chapter, Chapter 7, "Supplementary Provisions," acknowledges the special circumstances of "overseas schools, hospitals, scientific and engineering technology research institutions or academic organizations" that "engage in exchange and cooperation activities" with similar Chinese institutions. These are to be administered through state regulations already established for them, except when such institutions are in violation of Art. 5 which, as we have seen, establishes the framework of China's public security concerns, with which all overseas NGOs must comply, including specific prohibitions against engaging in or funding "for-profit activities or political activities," and illegally conducting or funding "religious activities" (Art. 53).

*

The bottom line in the "Law on the Management of the Activities of Overseas NGOs within Mainland China" is that such NGOs have only two paths towards achieving the compliance that would enable them to carry out charitable activities in China legally. They must either (1) establish a representative office and pass the indicated procedure for registration, or (2) they must cooperate with an approved CPO and file a report of their temporary activities before engaging in them. In either case, their registration and/or report must first be approved by a "Professional Supervisory Unit (PSU) (业务主管单位)" (Art. 6), before it can be submitted for final approval.

If the second option is chosen, it requires establishing a proper relationship with an approved CPO and filing an annual report of "temporary activities," to be certified by the CPO before submitting it to the PSU and the appropriate regulatory agency for final approval. Any changes in the reported "temporary activities" must be documented and similarly submitted for approval. It is clear, then, that this second option is not to be regarded as a workaround for unregistered overseas NGOs. Given the rigorous procedures stipulated under either option, overseas NGOs that have the resources to establish a representative office in China, and can comply with the two-step process for registering it, by all means, should do so.

While the level of documentation required under the Overseas NGO Law may seem burdensome to some foreign observers, everyone must recognize China's sovereign right to impose such regulations, and the wisdom of offering a comprehensive package of regulations in response to well-documented public security issues that have arisen because of the illegal activities of some overseas NGOs. As we shall see further on, though the enforcement of this new law only began on 1 January 2017, already a significant number of overseas NGOs previously operating in China have successfully passed the registration procedure in Beijing, Shanghai, and Guangdong. As more and more NGOs seek to comply with the new law, no doubt there will be ample opportunity for both them and the agencies regulating them to fine tune the law to render it more effective in fulfilling its stated and legitimate purposes.

3.3 Compliance Issues and How to Manage Them

Compliance requires coordination among government regulators, local charitable organizations, and overseas NGOs involved in charitable activities in China. Beyond a basic understanding of the new laws — as outlined in previous two chapters — compliance requires each of these institutional sectors to implement them in a timely fashion. Because of the unprecedented level of change involved in shifting to the new framework, it must be expected that there will be unanticipated problems at every level.

At this point, we can provide only a tentative report on how well the compliance process is working for all concerned. What follows is a summary of what we have learned so far. We will proceed, first, with a review of what is known about the work of both the Ministry of Civil Affairs' (MCA) management of local charitable organizations, and the Ministry of Public Security's management of overseas NGOs. Second, we will review the situation of local organizations directly accountable to the MCA. Third, we will review the same for overseas NGOs directly accountable to the MPS.

Observers have pointed out the dramatic increase in the number of NGOs operating in China today. According to official Chinese sources, there are roughly 7,000 overseas NGOs, while the number of registered social organizations is 675,000, consisting of 328,000 social associations, 342,000 social service organizations, and 5,204 foundations. There are, as well, an estimated 3 million unregistered social organizations in China (Brookings Institute, 2016). Trying to achieve compliance among so many organizations amounts to a regulatory "Great Leap Forward ... arguably the biggest legislative development in the history of the non-profit sector in the PRC" (International Center for Not-for-Profit Law (ICNL), 2017).

3.3.1　Regulating Charitable Organizations Through the Ministry of Civil Affairs (MCA)

To facilitate the registration and reporting process outlined in the new Charity Law, the MCA has issued several directives clarifying the legal status of "charitable organizations" (慈善组织, *cishan zuzhi*) in relation to previously recognized categories of social organizations (CSOs). Any of these — namely, Social Associations (SAs), Social Service Organizations (SSOs), and Foundations — can also apply for "charitable organization" status, provided they meet the criteria outlined in the Charity Law (Arts. 3 and 9).

- On 1 August 2016, the MCA posted the "Amendment of the Regulation on Registration and Management of Social Organizations" online for public consideration. This directive clarifies which government bodies are responsible, the registration requirements and procedures, the internal governance of the organization, their legal responsibilities, among other things.
- On 29 August 2016, the MCA issued "The Measures for the Designation of Charitable Organizations" and "The Measures on the Administration of Public Fund-raising by Charitable Organizations." These are meant to facilitate establishing charitable organization status, so that CSOs engaged in charitable activities can qualify for certain benefits, such as the extension of public fund-raising credentials.
- On 11 October 2016, the MCA and Ministry of Finance and State Administration of Taxation issued "Regulations on the Annual

Expenditures and Management Expenses of Charitable Organizations Carrying Out Charitable Activities," following up on the guidelines established in Art. 60 of the Charity Law.

Clearly, the MCA's follow-up guidelines are meant to encourage Chinese CSOs to register and comply with the Charity Law, while also assuring all stakeholders that the bulk of funds donated to these organizations are spent on charitable activities.

3.3.1.1 *Regulating Overseas NGOs through the Ministry of Public Security (MPS)*

While the Charity Law went into effect on 1 September 2016, the Overseas NGO Law came into force on 1 January 2017. Staggering their dates of enforcement allowed the MPS to establish its regulatory procedures, a task for which it had not been responsible previously. On 14 October 2016, the MPS and the Shanghai Public Security Bureau (PSB) held a news conference in Shanghai, outlining the process of registering either an overseas NGO's representative offices or its temporary activities, in the dual supervision system involving both Professional Supervisory Units (PSUs) and the provincial MPS (Arts. 40 and 41).

- The Shanghai PSB, therefore, detailed how its "Entry/Exit Administration" had already set up booths, signs, and equipment to receive overseas NGOs, and other provinces and cities are reportedly preparing their own service stations. In addition, the Shanghai PSB was constructing an "overseas NGO management service information system and websites," so that these organizations can access "online platforms to make reservations for registration or filing of records, make online applications and submissions of relevant materials, and post relevant documents."
- On 28 November, the MPS released the official "Guidelines on Organizational Registration and Temporary Activities Reporting under the Overseas NGO Law" (境外非政府组织代表机构登记和临时活动备案办事指南). While these Guidelines have no legal force as such, they do represent an effort by the MPS to provide a clearer explanation of what it will take to achieve compliance with the law. To facilitate its two-step registration and reporting system, on 20 December, the MPS

released the official directory of PSUs for the relevant fields and sectors.

3.3.1.2 *Chinese Charitable Organizations and their Responses*

While much has been reported about the process of achieving compliance with the Overseas NGO Law, at this point there is very little discussion on the responses of the local Chinese NGOs to the Charity Law. This is not surprising, given the massive number of such organizations. Many of these have successfully registered as for-profit businesses, even though they are engaged in various "charitable activities" as listed in Art. 3 of the Charity Law. They opted for registration as businesses because at the time it was relatively easier to obtain such a registration — the documentation required being less burdensome — and, so long as local authorities were satisfied that indeed their activities resulted in a public benefit, and were not involved in any of the prohibited activities listed in the law (Arts. 4 and 5), their ambiguous status was generally tolerated.

Given that the Charity Law now provides a comprehensive regulatory framework, clearly intended to facilitate the growth of legitimate Chinese charitable organizations, while also establishing clear guidelines for achieving transparency and accountability in fund-raising, the recruitment and management of volunteers as well as paid staff, and delivery of services — as well as the penalties for noncompliance with the law — it seems clear that eventually even grassroots NGOs in China will achieve compliance with the law.

3.3.1.3 *Overseas NGOs and their Responses*

Even though primary responsibility for regulating overseas NGOs has been shifted to the MPS for the first time, the challenge of achieving compliance appears to be far less difficult than that faced by the MCA in regulating grassroots NGOs.

- By the end of January 2017, the MPS announced that twenty NGOs in Beijing, and six NGOs in Guangdong, had received their registration certificates. By the beginning of April, China's official platform for overseas NGOs reported that 62 had received registration approvals for their representative offices in 23 provinces, districts, and cities, while another 170 had applied to their proper PSUs and were therefore being processed.

- As Shawn Shieh reported, the initial batch of successfully registered NGOs included "familiar names like the World Economic Forum, Save the Children, the Bill and Melinda Gates Foundation, and the Paulson Foundation. The Guangdong NGOs include "the Hong Kong Chinese General Chamber of Commerce (Guangzhou), the Federation of Hong Kong Industries (Shenzhen), and the Taiwan Trade Center (Guangzhou)." Generally, the successful registrants were overseas NGOs that "had already been registered as representative offices of foundations under the Ministry of Civil Affairs."

- The first six overseas NGOs that registered a representative office in Shanghai included "Project HOPE — Health Opportunity for People Everywhere" (世界健康基金会), the Hong Kong Yin Shin Leung Charitable Foundation (香港应善良基金会), the US–China Business Council (美国美中贸易全国委员会), the Canada China Business Council (加拿大加中贸易理事会), the Russian Federation Chamber of Commerce and Industry (俄罗斯联邦工商会), and the Confederation of Indian Industry (上海代表处和印度工业联合会)" (Shieh, 2017).

- While most of these organizations are not involved in charitable activities, the fact that some charitable organizations have successfully been registered indicates that the compliance process is functional, even though clearly riddled with difficulties for less well-established organizations whose mission may be regarded as politically sensitive.

It is important to recognize that overseas NGOs, like foreign businesses operating in China, are more visible, more subject to scrutiny by regulators and other stakeholders, and hence more vulnerable to sanctions, if they fail to achieve compliance with the law. Under such circumstances, just as some businesses at one time or another have decided to abandon their operations in China, so some overseas NGOs are reported weighing whether their presence in China has now become unsustainable. The discussion among them has often led to an either/or choice: either go or stay, either abandon their mission in China or allow the MPS's regulations to redefine their mission, to the point that they become marginalized.

Nevertheless, this either/or choice is falsely posed. There is no evidence that the intent of the law is to force overseas NGOs to leave

China. Nor is a merely passive response to the MPS's registration and reporting requirements the only other alternative.

One way forward — as the University of Nottingham's Andreas Fulda suggested — is "for foreign NPOs to adopt a strategy of 'smart indigenisation'," which consists of working closely with Chinese CSOs including the "more than 5,000 Chinese private foundations operating within the country." Such partnerships would have to be formed after due diligence prior to petitioning the relevant PSUs for permission to apply for certification of the overseas NGO's "temporary activities" in China. Chinese foundations — for example, One Foundation, Narada Foundation, China Foundation for Poverty Alleviation as well as the SEE Foundation — could become "natural partners for those foreign NPOs which are keen to continue their collaboration with Chinese civil society organisations, albeit in an indirect way" (Fulda, 2017).

In Chapter 4, we will explore this suggestion and other constructive responses to the new laws, in the hope of supporting the further development of corporate philanthropy in China.

Chapter 4

The Wisdom of Experience: Striving Towards a Proper Alignment

4.1. In Search of Practical Advice

Rothlin Ltd's Corporate Philanthropy Project (CPP) included several in-depth interviews with representatives of foreign and local businesses, as well as foreign and local non-governmental organizations (NGOs), involved in philanthropic activities in China. While their perspectives on Chinese philanthropy differed in detail — not surprisingly in describing the challenges that their organizations face — a consensus among them is evident in their views on what must be done to improve the effectiveness of their overall performance in meeting the needs of Chinese people. We will first outline the challenges faced by these groups and then attempt to discern the best practices commonly advocated by them.

4.1.1 The Challenges: Foreign Business Perspectives

Conventional approaches to philanthropy that "usually give money away without asking what is going to happen" cannot and should not be sustained. As one informant indicated, "We cannot just give the money to NGOs or send it to the village directly. We have to be on the ground and see where the money is going and with what results." Effective philanthropy must aim higher than doing good things or merely looking good. Though philanthropy may seem like just another form of investment, it cannot be reduced to questions of financial transfers — donations given, donations received — but must be understood as developing relationships in which various interests, including the business' own purpose, are harmonized. "It is a balance thing. How do you balance self-interest with goodness?" The challenge is reciprocal and will involve demanding changes not only of philanthropies funded by businesses, but also of the businesses' own corporate cultures. Transparency and accountability must become mutual, which means establishing relations of trust among all parties involved.

Building relations of trust requires foreign businesses in China to recognize the need to find and support partnerships with local NGOs. This involves exercising due diligence in evaluating the partners' potential for long-term collaboration and development, with extensive and intensive background checks. But once the partnership has been initiated, it also involves learning how to build up the partners' capacity for transparency and accountability, so that with appropriate transfer of administrative skills, the local NGO may become professionalized, establishing management routines that will enable them to respond effectively to their donors' inquiries. The challenge is for businesses to be willing to assist their local NGO partners to develop adequate financial controls that will help them qualify for further grants in an ongoing relationship.

4.1.2 The Challenges: Local Business Perspectives

A major challenge for local businesses seeking to get involved in philanthropic activities is learning how to do it, while minimizing the problems that such involvement may create for their own business growth and development. Building relationships of mutual trust, transparency, and accountability may be time-consuming and difficult to reconcile with the firm's entrepreneurial culture. Under such circumstances, if local businesses are serious about philanthropy, they, too, may be challenged to develop partnerships with intermediary agencies that can facilitate the development of relationships between philanthropic NGOs and local businesses. They may even consider innovative projects, such as establishing a foundation or a philanthropic incubator to assist the development of local NGOs by transferring skills in professionalized management. As one informant observed, one of the major problems of Chinese NGOs is that unprofessional people manage an unprofessional organization, which cannot develop in a bigger scope.

4.1.3 The Challenges: Foreign NGO Perspectives

Foreign NGOs are often found at the center of relationship building between businesses seeking to become donors or supporters of local philanthropic organizations and recipients seeking to develop such organizations. Since every foreign NGO has its own history, and its own specific area of expertise — for example, addressing the needs of children, or environmental concerns, or poverty reduction, or promoting rural education, or any of the other charitable activities recognized as legitimate by law in China — the challenges they face are likely to be specific to these areas. Nevertheless, their insights deepen our understanding of what it means to cultivate relations of trust with local charitable organizations. As one informant observed, "in 9 out of 10 cases, the local organization may have much more knowledge of specific needs" in the community, even if the donor organizations may have more professional expertise in a certain field. If trust is to be sustained, the asymmetry in knowledge must be acknowledged and respected. "It's wrong if a project is donor-driven instead of needs-driven," meaning that the foreign NGO must learn to cultivate effective partnerships with local organizations that have the relevant knowledge.

A major challenge for foreign NGOs is achieving compliance with the new laws regulating their activities in China. Among our informants from this group, the nature of this challenge may be understood in different ways. One key term used to describe it is "alignment." How is the Foreign NGO aligned in its values and its potential contributions in China, not only with its local partners or recipient organizations, but also with various government agencies? In the past some foreign NGOs have been well aligned with provincial and local administrative units, but now they face the challenge of compliance with the new laws nationally, which require registry and supervision through the Ministry for Public Security (MPS). Others, however, for many years may have been properly aligned with the Ministry of Civil Affairs (MCA) but now face new challenges of compliance with the MPS regulatory framework. In either case, compliance is essential if the foreign NGOs are to sustain their work in China.

4.1.4 The Challenges: Local NGOs Perspectives

Local NGOs involved in philanthropic activities, because they are local, usually are responding to specific needs within the communities they serve.

Often, they are in competition with other organizations, not only for the support of donors, but also for recognition by the relevant regulatory agencies that must certify their registration and compliance with relevant laws. The alignment challenge for local NGOs may also involve their complex histories of sponsorship and involvement with foreign businesses and NGOs, which may either enable or impede their future development. Representatives of the local NGOs we have studied are acutely aware of the need to professionalize their management to facilitate the development of their relationships not only with government regulators but also with donors, both foreign and local. While none of them indicated that the challenge of building trust through greater transparency and accountability was inappropriate, they did indicate that they were often lacking in the resources needed to achieve full compliance with all the demands made upon them.

4.1.5 The Challenges: Learning From Hong Kong?

One of our informants is involved with a very successful local NGO in Hong Kong. His insights suggest that the situation for philanthropic activities there is very different from that usually experienced in mainland China. Typically, there is close cooperation between the Hong Kong government and NGOs both local and foreign in identifying unmet local needs and in engaging philanthropic resources to address them. Philanthropy, in his view, is an accepted part of entrepreneurial culture in Hong Kong, where successful entrepreneurs compete for status and public recognition as philanthropists. There are awards and other tokens of appreciation that motivate a high level of philanthropic involvement by business leaders in Hong Kong, which our informant believes should also be institutionalized in mainland China. The challenge for China is to develop the new laws governing philanthropic activities so that the regulatory agencies may serve, not simply as compliance officers, but as senior partners working with both businesses and NGOs to address the needs of the Chinese peoples. If the challenge uniting all perspectives is the building of mutually beneficial relationships of trust, transparency, and accountability within and among all participating organizations, the government clearly must do all it can to ensure that its agencies play a positive role in fostering that development.

4.1.6 Recommended Best Practices

- However different the challenges faced may be, the path towards concrete and practical solutions seems more like a broad and well-marked highway than a series of individual trails meandering through an unfamiliar forest. The broad highway has a clear destination: build partnerships with local organizations by establishing mutual trust at all levels.

- How to establish mutual trust may require experimenting with a variety of strategies. Foreign NGOs may build a good reputation in China, by making themselves useful to various stakeholders — local NGOs, businesses both foreign and local, and government regulatory agencies. One such strategy is providing training programs that enable such stakeholders to professionalize their administrative practices and thus participate more effectively. Another is to identify experienced advisors who have the local knowledge, who can serve as consultants as an organization develops its philanthropic activities. Still another is to cultivate a collaborative relationship with local government agencies, if possible, making them mentors who will help an organization identify their priorities among local needs and tailor their involvement accordingly.

- Identifying local partners, of course, requires due diligence. There is no substitute for doing the research necessary to understand the background and the performance histories of the likely partners and stakeholders. Given the previous lack of transparency and public accountability of many Chinese philanthropic organizations, due diligence will have to be done discreetly and with an appropriate degree of mutual respect and understanding. There is no room for prejudice in an effective due diligence process. Arbitrary biases either for or against individual stakeholders inevitably are counterproductive.

- Once a partnership is established, there must be adequate planning that maps out how the relationship is expected to develop. The terms of the collaboration should be spelt out in a memorandum of understanding (MOU), specifying each of the mutual expectations and promises, and addressing the foreseeable contingencies that may have an impact, positively or negatively, on the fulfillment of these expectations.

- If funds are to be transferred from a donor to a recipient organization, the process of transfer must be compliant with the relevant sections of the new laws governing local charities and/or the activities of foreign NGOs in China.

- Beyond meeting the government's compliance requirements, donors and recipients should formally agree to a schedule of fund transfers, for example, a certain portion of the grant might be withheld until a later date, after a review of the funded activities is completed to both parties' mutual satisfaction. One of our informants suggested that a three-year funding cycle with annual reviews to monitor progress had been very effective in keeping projects on track.

- Good planning for increased transparency and accountability is a two-way street. Local NGOs that receive support from donors, either foreign or local, must take care to produce timely reports explaining the status of the project, successes achieved, and obstacles to be overcome, so that the donors' level of trust can be enhanced. A regular reporting schedule should not be left as an afterthought, nor should it be treated casually. The future of their relationship with donors depends on the quality of the reports they issue regularly.

- Building a partnership based on mutual trust, of course, will require all the parties involved to recognize the asymmetrical character of their relationship. The asymmetries concern access to resources and local knowledge, obviously; but also certain intangibles such as cultural background, organizational complexity, previous experience in China, and relationships with other stakeholders such as government regulatory agencies, etc. Each of these asymmetries may create its own challenges in seeking to achieve "balance" or a proper alignment between or among partners. It is therefore very useful if the planning process identifies these asymmetries in advance, and anticipates the kinds of responses that can turn them from obstacles into opportunities for growth. Successfully weathering a challenge that is well understood by the partners is likely to ensure a more reliable basis for future collaboration.

- The partners in any philanthropic activity must examine their attitudes towards the new laws and governmental agencies supervising them. Similarly, government regulatory agencies must examine their own attitudes towards philanthropic organizations. Compliance with the law will not be enough to keep a partnership on track if the partners fail to recognize and open themselves to direction and assistance from the government. By the same token, government agencies can undermine their own missions if they approach the task of regulation with an adversarial attitude implying that all concerned are trying to evade public scrutiny.

- As we have attempted to show in the previous chapters, outlining the provisions of the new laws, and their various requirements, provide a model of how to achieve transparency and accountability. Though some of the provisions may have to be revised, if they turn out to be ineffective for various reasons, there can be no doubt that the government is mandating comprehensive standards of transparency and accountability for all organizations involved in philanthropic activities, including the government agencies that regulate them. If the reforms mandated in the new laws are embraced by all stakeholders, and a good faith effort is made to implement them, philanthropic organizations will already have made substantial progress in adopting best practices in this field.

4.2 The Wisdom of Experience: Avoiding Preventable Mistakes

As in the previous section, here we will attempt to summarize insights derived from several in-depth interviews with representatives of foreign and local businesses, as well as foreign and local NGOs, involved in philanthropic activities in China. We have described the challenges highlighted by our informants. We also identified certain best practices for building and sustaining relationships of mutual trust, transparency, and accountability in partnerships between philanthropic donors and recipients. In this section, the focus shifts to avoiding preventable mistakes. What can be said about the ways in which a relationship can get sidetracked, stalled, or broken, and what, if anything can be done to correct it? We will make general observations about bad habits in need of correction, and then offer recommendations for moving forward.

4.2.1 Overcoming Bad Habits: Foreign Businesses' Perspectives

Living and working abroad inevitably requires a certain degree of attitude adjustment. The learning curve involved is often referred to as "Culture Shock," and it is important to acknowledge that even a well-travelled expatriate can fall into attitudes towards local people that are chauvinistic and patronizing. These may range from unintended cultural slights to overtly abusive behaviours that are invariably counterproductive, especially if the challenge is to build a relationship of mutual trust that will enable both managers and staff, or in this case, donors and recipients, to collaborate effectively.

Our informants stressed the need to understand their own dependence on others for local knowledge, indispensable for identifying local needs as well as local resources required to respond effectively to them. Learning to listen well to one's local partners inevitably summons from us virtues rarely identified with business success, as we must find a balance between humility, patience, and empathy while being very firm and very clear in dealing with local partners. Representatives of foreign businesses engaged in developing collaborative relationships with local organizations are well advised to examine their "people skills," recognizing that success will result not from manipulation or intimidation, but from creating both the impression and the reality of sincerity. One place to begin to overcome one's bad habits in China would be to learn from the wisdom traditions of Chinese philosophy, especially the Confucian arts of self-cultivation. They still have much to teach us about how to become a true friend of the Chinese people.

The typical foreign business environment creates pressures that may become obstacles blocking the success of any philanthropic activities: An emphasis on short-term results, a reliance on the numbers or other impersonal measures of success, however useful for achieving internal performance goals, may turn out to be counterproductive when implemented in relations with local agencies and organizations. While building trust may be the goal, there clearly are policies and practices, however well-intended, that may undermine it. If mishandled in ways that are culturally insensitive, due diligence and rigorous adherence to accountability procedures, for example, may create the impression that local partners are likely to be blamed for anything and everything that goes wrong.

One frequently cited instance is blaming grant recipients for a project's failure or its delayed completion, when the government agency managing the grant has diverted the funds to another project. In the past this has happened often, and both the local NGOs as well as their donors have not been informed about the reallocation of funds or the reasons for it. The locals must explain to the donors what they did with the grant money, and their excuse may seem lame or incredible. Being unaware of the intricacies of a local NGO's relationships with various government agencies, the corporate donor may simply assume that the money was lost or stolen, resulting in a serious loss of face for the recipient. It is hoped that the new laws will minimize the frequency of such situations by mandating clear standards of accountability for the relevant government regulatory agencies as well as for the NGOs and businesses involved in philanthropic activities.

Face saving, however, is not a uniquely Chinese cultural phenomenon. Foreign business corporations are as acutely concerned about their reputations as Chinese people traditionally have been about saving face. Companies may be too focused on identifying local projects that make for good photo opportunities — such as helping school children with their lessons or refurbishing rural school buildings — rather than responding to the underlying challenges identified by their local NGO advisors. Even if corporate donors are sincere in their desire to help, they may create the impression that their chief interest is in doing a photo shoot for the next annual report.

A related issue concerns the corporate tendency towards self-protection. Businesses that work with local NGOs to identify and respond to local needs may become aware that the products — say, the manufacture and sale of pesticides — they are promoting in China are creating health problems in the areas where they operate. Once aware of their possible involvement, some businesses have been known to focus their concerns elsewhere, rather than risk raising questions about their overall business plan. But one's philanthropic concerns, if sincere, should motivate a company to make a top priority of correcting its own practices. Respecting local cultures, it may also be necessary to make sure that public apologies will be perceived as truly genuine and respectful. Corporate philanthropy is not a fig-leaf or a veil for covering up corporate mistakes, abuses, and the unintended consequences — "externalities," as economists might describe them — of their business operations.

4.2.2 Overcoming Bad Habits: Foreign NGOs

Foreign NGOs like foreign businesses must adhere to the highest standards of business ethics, in all aspects of their operations, if they are to sustain their credibility as partners in the development of Chinese philanthropy. As our informants indicated, to put it bluntly they are being watched.

They should try to turn the heightened scrutiny they face — from the public at large, from bloggers, journalists, and the news media, as well as from government regulators — into an opportunity to model best business practices. Their good example may be the best contribution they can make to Chinese philanthropy. Foreign NGOs often function as intermediaries, advising both foreign and local businesses, local NGOS, and government agencies, as well as facilitating the development of working relationships among them all. As intermediaries, they are likely to be challenged with the persistence of corruption among Chinese institutions. Bribery, from whatever source, or however significant its alleged benefits, must never be tolerated. Foreign NGOs must lead the way in establishing compliance with China's new laws governing philanthropic activity. In China, as elsewhere, they must be part of the solution, not part of the problem.

As intermediaries, foreign NGOs may serve as repositories of wisdom and experience regarding local problems and the track record of local agencies in addressing them. They must be prepared to say "No" to schemes for helping children and other vulnerable people that are inappropriate and not well grounded in Chinese cultural practices and local knowledge. The NGOs must try to negotiate with well-intentioned donors, steering them towards projects and partners that promise to be effective in meeting local needs. Among the challenges they will face is the development of a realistic time frame in which to measure results, and other mutually agreed upon accountability routines. Their advice in such matters will be persuasive only to the extent that their integrity is generally known and respected.

When their local partners fail to meet mutually agreed upon goals, foreign NGOs will be challenged to respond in ways that seek to overcome difficulties without creating a breach in the relationship of trust they have established. There is no quick and easy solution to such problems. Our informants agree that it makes no sense simply to ignore problems while hoping for a better future. Transparency may be the key to accountability, but it cannot be imposed unilaterally without risking increased levels of mistrust and resentment.

Sometimes an intervention will be necessary, but its focus should be developmental, that is, it must seek to develop the organizational capabilities of local partners, the transfer of management skills and accountability structures, which will make future success more likely. The relationships between foreign donors and local recipients are likely to be asymmetrical, for all the reasons indicated in previous chapters. Those who would respond effectively to institutional asymmetries in China are well advised to master the philosophy of *wú wéi* (无为) as outlined in the *Book of Changes* or *Yijing* (易經). *Wú wéi* urges us to abstain from hasty interventions, while cultivating an ability to wait until the critical point is reached, when mutual objectives can be achieved without creating further difficulties. Interventions, in short, must never be heavy-handed; but must take advantage of every opportunity to restore a trustful harmony, continually moving things along in the path of least resistance to the fulfillment of one's goals.

4.2.3 Overcoming Bad Habits: Local Businesses and NGOs

Seeking out partnerships with philanthropic organizations is inevitably transformative. Old ways of doing things will no longer be sufficient either for mere survival, or for steady growth and development. Local NGOs will be challenged to develop a greater sense of clarity about their mission, their specific goals, and the kinds of assistance they require to meet them. It simply will not do to merely land a donor, any donor with cash on hand. Alignment is a complex process that involves converging cultural values as well as matching technical capabilities. An increase in paperwork and so-called "red tape is predictable, thus demanding the development of adequate policies for record keeping, filing timely reports to donors and government agencies, managing paid staff and volunteers, and providing them with the resources needed to carry out their responsibilities — in short, partnerships will inevitably lead to professionalized management.

One important management challenge is fulfilling mutually agreed upon expectations. If donors earmark their funds for specific projects, the funds must be used for those projects, and accounted for as such. Earmarked donations cannot simply be deposited into a general account and used to pay bills, responding to whatever needs may come along, even if these seem to have a greater priority than the purpose for which the donation was given. At the very least, if there is any repurposing of funds already donated, the organization must inform, if not obtain the permission, of the donors. It is good to know that the new Charity Law is very clear on this point, and stipulates procedures to ensure that all donations are adequately accounted for.

4.2.4 Overcoming Bad Habits: Government Agencies

The history of 20th century philanthropy in China reflects changes that occurred in the context of a struggle against foreign colonial interference. Though China has emerged from this struggle with impressive successes in the era of economic and social reform, mistakes were made and their negative impact lingers. Many Chinese people became cynical about local charitable organizations, which gave them reasons to withdraw their support for charitable activities. This basic distrust not only has impeded the government's efforts at public welfare, but also slowed the development of private philanthropy. China's new laws governing charitable organizations both foreign and local should not be regarded as more of the same.

Our analysis indicates that the laws are a good faith effort to extend the rule of law to all charitable institutions as well as to the government agencies that supervise their activities. But for them to succeed in their purpose, the attitude of distrust must be overcome. They must be given the benefit of the doubt. Strategies of evasion must give way to a new era of public–private cooperation, as some of our informants have pointed out. Significantly, the new laws contain provisions for monitoring and disciplining agencies that regulate charitable institutions so that patterns of corruption so pervasive in the past can be overcome. All institutions, foreign and local, businesses as well as NGOs, if not already registered and compliant with the laws, must do so, and as soon as possible. We are convinced that China's philanthropic sector will grow dramatically, once past attitudes of distrust and cynicism are set aside, for the sake of the common good.

4.3 Philanthropy and Confucian Entrepreneurship: A Way Forward?

The generosity of ordinary Chinese people, now enjoying resources that could be devoted to charitable activities, has been well demonstrated by their response to major disasters, like the Wenchuan earthquake in 2008. But that generosity was undercut by widespread distrust of philanthropic organizations — private and public — that lingered in the wake of the so-called Red Cross scandal of 2011. We therefore decided that our contribution should focus on relationship-building, highlighting the role of personal and institutional efforts to create the conditions of mutual trust through increased transparency and accountability.

As our informants suggest, the conditions for building mutual trust include a rudimentary understanding of China's history of philanthropy, which would make us appreciate the wisdom of traditional Chinese practices and provide suggestions on how to reconnect to the Chinese approach to philanthropy, a thorough familiarity with China's new laws governing charitable activities and organizations, a commitment not only to compliance, but also to active collaboration with the government agencies seeking to establish a comprehensive framework for regulating and promoting them, and a willingness to learn the lessons of experience from persons and organizations that have helped to develop China's philanthropic organizations over the years. But beyond all these, we must also emphasize the importance of Chinese values that support our common human impulse towards helping those in need. Education in Chinese moral philosophy is indispensable for building trust, and the need for such education should be felt equally among local as well foreign NGOs and businesses. Without such education, philanthropical offers of friendship to China are likely to ring hollow.

Confucian entrepreneurship, of course, is no substitute for superior skills in business administration, and will not make up for failures in social innovation. But it does restore the challenge of imagining and implementing the common good to its rightful place, at the centre of enterprise development. One indication of the promise of Confucian entrepreneurship is the response of a small but growing number of Chinese philanthropists, who, since 2010, have signed "The Giving Pledge" proposed and organized by Bill Gates and Warren Buffet.

Confucian entrepreneurship, naturally, ought to be at the centre of restoring China's philanthropic culture. What makes entrepreneurship Confucian is its positive relationship to Confucian wisdom, which has always maintained a moral distinction between right ways and wrong ways of acquiring resources and managing wealth. Confucian values, of course, were specifically cited in Dr. Tsu Yu Yue's analysis of *The Spirit of Chinese Philanthropy* (1912), showing how its conception of moral virtue is rooted in a natural sympathy for others, a root that can bear fruit not only personally, but in a culture of social and institutional practices that will support philanthropy. Consistent with Dr. Tsu's perspective, the vision of the Ideal Commonwealth State (*dàtóng*: 大同) outlined in the *Book of Rites* (*Liji*: 礼记) is still deeply inspiring.

In the "Lǐ Yùn" chapter (礼运) of the *Book of Rites*, Confucius describes *dàtóng* as a perfect state in which all persons achieve fulfillment in all things material and spiritual, hence an "ideal commonwealth state." While admitting that he has never seen such a state, Confucius holds out a realistic hope for its inevitably partial and incomplete realization in a *xiǎokāng* (小康), that is, a reasonably prosperous state referred to as "the small tranquillity." During the era of economic and social reform, the *xiǎokāng* once again is widely discussed by Chinese government officials and scholars. A reasonably prosperous state would be one in which philanthropy has popular support, as society attempts to address the problems caused by poverty, lack of access to quality education, as well as social and economic inequality. In Confucius' view, the *xiǎokāng* can be achieved if China's leaders act sincerely as moral leaders, that is, if they are "attentive to the rules of propriety, thus to secure the display of righteousness, the realization of sincerity, the exhibition of errors, the exemplification of benevolence, and the discussion of courtesy, showing the people all the normal virtues" (Lǐ Yùn, 2). If, inspired by their leaders' example, the people take to heart "all the normal virtues," the problems of distrust that impede the development of Chinese philanthropy will be overcome.

There is no doubt that China can make progress towards creating a *xiǎokāng* if business leaders, both foreign and domestic, seek to embody the values distinctive of Confucian entrepreneurship. Confucian entrepreneurs readily acknowledge the indispensable role of supporting philanthropic activities and organizations as a sign of one's sincerity (*chéng*: 誠, 诚) in following the Way of Confucius in all things. We recognize the ideals of Confucian entrepreneurship as convergent with our own commitment to the common good, in friendship with the Chinese people inspired by the example of Matteo Ricci (*Li Madou*: 利玛窦). However lofty the ideals that animate us, we believe these can be partially realized through practical measures such as those outlined in this chapter. But our focus cannot remain fixed on China alone. We need to learn from others, especially from European traditions of philanthropy. In the chapters that follow, we will examine some European traditions in the hope of deepening our Dialogue with China focused in this volume on philanthropy.

Part III
Survey of Philanthropy in Europe

Chapter 5

Philanthropy in Europe: An Overview[*]

5.1 The World's Major Associations of Foundations

Over the last two to three decades,[1] the number of foundations in the world has increased rapidly. To cope with this flourishing philanthropy sector, several major associations of foundations have been established in Europe and in the United States (US). The most renowned foundations' associations in the world are the European Foundation Centre (EFC), the Donors and Foundations Networks in Europe (DAFNE), the Foundation Centre in New York, and the Worldwide Initiatives for Grantmaker Support (WINGS) based in Sao Paulo of Brazil.

5.1.1 The European Foundation Centre

The European Foundation Centre, with over 25 years of experience and an initial group of seven founding members, has grown to become a more-than-200-member organization today. "The EFC is the platform for and champion of institutional philanthropy — with a focus on Europe, but also with an eye to the global philanthropy landscape." The EFC is headquartered in Brussels, Belgium; it supports its members in their work — both

---

*This chapter was originally published in Ling Ji and Christoph Stückelberger (2017). *Foundation Management, China Christian Series.* Geneva: Globethics Publications.
[1] For this chapter, we especially acknowledge sources and data provided from *Observatoire de la Fondation de France, and Fondation 1796* (Lombard Odier Darier Hentsch).

individually and collectively — to foster positive social change in Europe and beyond.

The EFC analyses trends and issues within the sector and explores the wider context in which foundations operate. It also analyses European Union (EU) policy and regulatory frameworks to promote issues and influence policy from this perspective. The EFC's work is guided by three key questions: What is the role of foundations in building trust in society? How do foundations contribute to improving policy solutions and their implementation? How do the foundations work together to advance the well-being of their sector?

5.1.2 The Donors and Foundations Networks in Europe

The Donors and Foundations Networks in Europe is a network of 25 donors and foundations networks from across Europe, with a collective membership of over 7,500 foundations (Figure 5.1). According to the DAFNE website, "DAFNE underpins individual activities of its members

Global Philanthropy Networks
• Africa Grantmakers' Affinity Group
• Africa Philanthropy Network
• African Venture Philanthropy Alliance
• Ariadne Network
• Asia Venture Philanthropy Network
• Caribbean Philanthropy Network
• EDGE Funders
• European Venture Philanthropy Association
• Global Governance Philanthropy Network (GGPN)
• Global Fund for Community Foundations
• Human Rights Funders Network (HRFN)
• International Funders for Indigenous People (IFIP)
• Latin American Venture Philanthropy Network (Latimpacto)
• Network of Engaged International Donors (NEID)
• Philanthropy for Climate
• Philanthropy Europe Association (Philea)
• Peace and Security Funders Group (PSFG)
• Worldwide Initiatives for Grantmaker Support (WINGS)

Figure 5.1.   Overview of major foundation networks.

Source: https://cof.org/page/philanthropic-infrastructure#global (accessed 7 November 2023).

by encouraging dialogue and collaboration between the national associations. Each DAFNE member individually serves public benefit foundations and other donors at the national level: their roles and services vary from country to country."[2]

This very diversity among DAFNE members themselves brings the opportunity of gaining different perspectives. Through DAFNE's activities, each member learns from their peers' experiences, enriches themselves, and gets to know the wider European context. From this angle, the DAFNE somehow creates a mechanism and platform for wider collaboration among European associations themselves; exchanges know-how between them; and creates a pool of knowledge at the level of the DAFNE network and among philanthropy support organizations.

As such, one can say that the DAFNE provides a collective voice for the foundations sector and their supporting membership associations in playing a representative role at the national level. The DAFNE also works with its two main strategic partners, the EFC and WINGS Foundation of the US, with the intention of strengthening the voice and representation of the philanthropic sector at both the European and global levels.[3]

The DAFNE provides for the following:

- exchanging national experiences;
- networking opportunities and encouraging joint projects and initiatives;
- promoting donor's best practices at EU level;
- supporting advocacy efforts at national, EU, and global levels;
- defining common positions on legal and fiscal issues; and
- data collection, consolidation, and analysis.

5.1.3 Foundation Centre of the USA

The Foundation Centre was established in 1956, and is headquartered in New York. According to the website of the Foundation Centre, it strives to be the leading source of information on global philanthropy. The Centre aims to connect people through data, analysis, and training; it maintains not only the most comprehensive database on the US but also

---

[2]http://www.dafne-online.eu.

[3]http://dafne-online.eu/about.

on global grant-makers. The Centre has become a robust, accessible knowledge bank for the philanthropy sector. The Centres' three main activities are: research, education, and training programmes that are intended for advancing knowledge on philanthropy at every level.

5.2 Historic Review of Philanthropy

Individual giving in all its forms is probably as old as human interaction. Fostered by the Judaeo-Christian tradition of charity, the Middle-Ages saw the birth of philanthropy, with the original dates of foundations in many European countries established in medieval times. In the West, giving, particularly private generosity, are associated with Anglo-Saxon and American cultures, where attitudes towards wealth are relatively relaxed. Private initiatives of transferring a part of one's wealth for the common good are not only an expression and act of religious faith, but also often seen as an integral part of one's relationship with one's community.[4] At the same time, Europe is a diverse continent and giving is conditioned by differences in history and culture, economic and political circumstances, and taxation rules. During the second half of the 20th century, four different models of philanthropy within the European continent have evolved:

- the Anglo-Saxon model, where civil society organizations (CSOs) are seen as a counter-weight to government;
- the Rhine model, which involves a form of "social corporatism" with CSOs, is often contracted by the state;
- the Mediterranean model, where the church is seen as responsible for charity; and
- the Scandinavian model, which is based on a strong welfare state, with a strong tradition of volunteering.

When the welfare state model was widespread in Europe after the World War II, particularly in Scandinavian countries, the states took responsibility not only for protecting citizens and developing

---

[4]Please refer "An Overview of Philanthropy in Europe," (Observatoire de la Fondation de France/CerPhi), April 2015; also see, "A Flourishing European Philanthropy Sector," (Fondation de France), June 2015. Also, the first presentation of the history of American philanthropy by a Chinese scholar, Zi Zhong Ju (2015), is very interesting.

infrastructure, but also in terms of healthcare, social security, and education. Philanthropy focused on complementary areas such as culture and religion.[5] Over the last two to three decades, with the advance of European wealth creation, philanthropy has been sustained and developed further; and it currently is redefining the role of private initiatives in the public arena.

5.3 Main Indicators of European and American Philanthropy

How does European philanthropy, taken as a whole, bear comparison with its American counterpart?

If we compare data on the donor population and total individual giving amounts, Europe comes after the United States. In Europe, 44.3% of the population are donors and the total amount of giving is €22.4 billion The total giving as a proportion of GDP is 0.2%. Whereas in the US 95.4% are donors for the total amount of €224 billion. The total giving as a proportion of GDP is 1.5%.[6] The donations must also be seen in relation to the social welfare state: In Europe, citizens pay more taxes for well-developed social security and the need for private social services is therefore lower than in the US where the social security is less developed and more private support is needed.

On the other hand, the newest data compiled by the DAFNE and the EFC and analysed by the Foundation Centre in New York indicate that there are more than 141,000 registered "public benefit foundations" in Europe, with combined annual expenditures of more than €56 billion; whereas there are about 104,107 registered "public benefit foundations" in the US with annual expenditures of €53.5 billion.

Table 5.1 illustrates that the philanthropic wealth (total foundation assets) in the US is much greater than in Europe, nevertheless, the foundation vitality index (expenditure-to-assets ratio) in Europe, at 12.9%, is much more dynamic than that of the US (8.6%). This can be explained by the fact that American foundations are largely capital appreciation or stock foundations, while the dominant and growing model in Europe is the foundation reliant on donation inflows.

---

[5] *Ibid.*
[6] *Ibid.*

Table 5.1.   Comparative indicators of European and American philanthropy.

Main Indicators	Europe	United States
Foundations		
Number (from 19 major European countries)	141,000	104,107
Total expenditure (from 13 European countries)	€56 billion	US$71 billion
Total assets (from 13 European countries)	€433 billion	US$823 billion
Vitality (expenditure-to-assets ratio)	12.9%	8.6%
Expenditure as proportion of GDP (9 European countries)	0.45%	0.45%
Individual Giving		
% of population as donors (10 European countries)	44.3%	95.4%
Individual giving total (9 European countries)	€24.4 billion	US$229 billion
Proportion of giving to GDP	0.2%	1.5%

Source: "An Overview of Philanthropy in Europe," (Observatoire de la Fondation de France/CerPhi), April 2015; also see, McGill, Lawrence T., "Number of Registered Public Benefit Foundations in Europe Exceeds 141,000," (Foundation Centre, 2015).

5.4   Measurement and Characteristics of European Philanthropy

The methodology for studying European philanthropy is still in its developing stages and is not yet standardized. Our objective in this chapter is to give practitioners an overall picture on philanthropy, in particular European philanthropy. To do so, we have chosen to adopt quantitative as well as qualitative data analyses for the selected 10 European countries, namely: Netherlands, UK, Germany, Switzerland, France, Poland, Italy, Belgium, Spain, and Sweden, where the philanthropy sector is relatively well developed. Based on available data on these 10 countries, we then discuss measurement, and characteristics of European philanthropy from the two principal aspects of philanthropy: individual giving and the public-benefit foundations sector.

5.4.1   Individual Giving

Giving means choosing a cause, an organization, or a beneficiary. It means contributing to a private initiative for the good of the greatest number. But it also and above all means:

(a) through the act of becoming a donor;
(b) deciding what should be of "general interest"; and
(c) aligning one's own personal vision to the definition of "general interest" and its implementation.

Based on our research, the behaviour of individual giving varies widely from one country to another, nevertheless, the priority causes for European individual giving behaviour are international solidarity, social welfare, and religion. The main causes supported in the different countries demonstrate different conceptions of solidarity. For example, *in France, giving for national causes is dominant*: French donors, like the Spanish, donate primarily for their own most vulnerable compatriots (37% of donations). *"For the Germans, Belgians and Swiss, international and humanitarian aid is the priority"* (74% of total German donations, 61% of Belgian donations, and 43% of Swiss donations). *In the Netherlands and United Kingdom, religion is the largest cause supported* by individual philanthropy and the largest motivation.[7]

"All European states now recognise the role of private philanthropy in works that benefit the public interest, as demonstrated by the introduction of tax incentive mechanisms (Sweden was the last country to introduce such a mechanism in 2012). Tax breaks encourage people who are already donors to increase the amount of their gift, rather than promoting the emergence of new donors. The French deductibility system is particularly advantageous for donors, compared to neighbouring European countries. In several countries, a proportion of tax is directly allocated to religion or the charity sector. In Germany, the church tax (*Kirchensteuer*) is added to any tax due at a rate of 8 to 9% of the tax due to the State."[8]

For assessing philanthropy and comparing national situations, the number of donors and the percentage they represent in a country's population are the foremost useful indicators. Figure 5.2 reveals which countries in Europe contribute the most in terms of their donor population as a whole. The data on individual donations includes the giving population as a percentage of the national population.

Figure 5.3 shows the breakdown of the giving amount in the 10 selected European countries (excluding Poland, for which data are

---

[7]"A Flourishing European Philanthropy Sector," Fondation de France, June 2015.
[8]"An Overview of Philanthropy in Europe," (Observatoire de la Fondation de France/ CerPhi), April 2015.

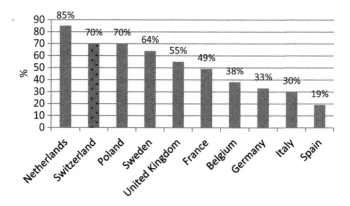

Figure 5.2. Proportion of donors by national population in Europe.

Source: "An Overview of Philanthropy in Europe," (Observatoire de la Fondation de France/CerPhi), April 2015.

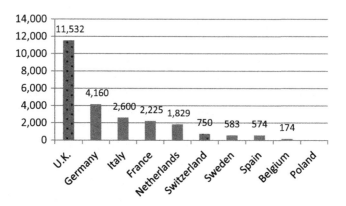

Figure 5.3. Individual giving amounts (in million euros).

Note: No data for Poland.
Source: "An Overview of Philanthropy in Europe" (Observatoire de la Fondation de France/CerPhi), April 2015.

not available). For all the nine European countries mentioned as a whole, philanthropy expressed in the form of individual giving totals more than €24.4 billion.

The estimated number of donors for each of these 10 European countries is illustrated in Figure 5.4, in which we can see the UK. "with an estimated donor population of almost 28 million, ranking the first; while France has the second largest number of donors with an estimated donor

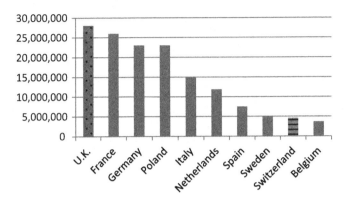

Figure 5.4.   Estimated number of donors.

Source: Observatoire de la Fondation de France/CerPhi, April 2015.

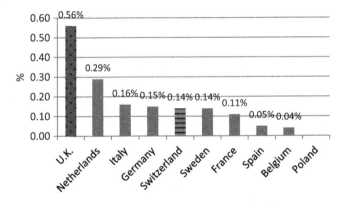

Figure 5.5.   Total individual giving as a proportion of GDP for 10 European countries.

Note: No data available for Poland.

Source: Observatoire de la Fondation de France/CerPhi, April 2015.

population of more than 25 million. Germany and Poland are next, with roughly similar estimated donor numbers of around 23 million."[9] If we sum-up figures for the 10 countries, the total number of donors is about 149 million people, representing 44.3% of the total population (Figure 5.5). These estimations are based on self-declared data and might not be exact; nevertheless, these figures serve as the useful and indicative value for measurement and show the characteristics of European philanthropy.

---

[9] *Ibid.*

5.4.2 Remarkable Rise of Foundations in Europe

The traditional foundation model is usually based on permanent funding from significant investment assets, the income of which is sufficient to support long-term philanthropic activity. The existence of large numbers of capital endowment foundations in the US and Europe represent a country's wealth, and the level of dedication to the causes of the social, cultural, and common good. Nevertheless, this is not the only face of foundations in Europe. In addition to this traditional mechanism of funding through capital endowment, two other phenomena in some European countries, namely, (1) *national lotteries* — collect colossal sums of money (€500 million in the Netherlands, €800 million in UK)[10]; and (2) fundraising events — crowd funding, for example — are setting a pace that is redefining the activities of donating money in the philanthropy sector. These new methods of giving are contributing to the evolution of giving behaviours and trends in Europe, which have stimulated the rise of foundations in Europe over the last two to three decades.

This boom of the fund and foundation sector in most European countries for the last 30 years indicates that the philanthropic culture is continuing to make progress. It is also due to the result of changes in the legal and fiscal frameworks of most European countries. As a result, huge numbers of small foundations have been created, a trend seen in several countries, such as community foundations focusing on local fund-raising, and foundations relying on incoming donations rather than capital, and so on. These smaller and younger foundations of Europe are dynamic and define themselves more in terms of their actions than their assets.

Beyond the remarkable rise of foundations in Europe from the perspectives of numbers (Figure 5.6), the economic weight in their respective national economies measured by foundation expenditure as a proportion of GDP is another characteristic of European foundations (Figure 5.7), that is, their vitality, which can be measured through their expenditure-to-assets ratio for these 10 European countries.

If we look at Figure 5.8, we can see that half the countries in Europe have a higher philanthropic vitality index than the US. Belgium, Spain, France, and Germany particularly stand out. From this figure, the mathematical calculation of average of expenditure-to-assets ratio is 18.1% for these 9 European countries (no data for Poland), this ratio is

---

[10] *Ibid.*

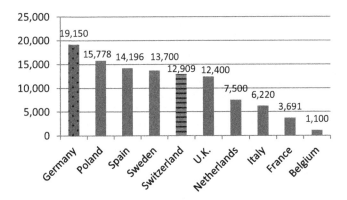

Figure 5.6.   Number of foundations in 10 European countries.

Source: Observatoire de la Fondation de France/CerPhi, April 2015.

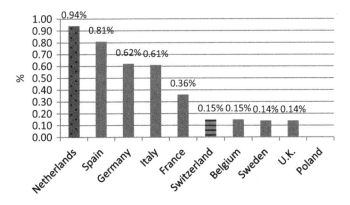

Figure 5.7.   Foundation expenditure as a proportion of GDP for 10 European countries.

Note: No data available for Poland.

Source: Observatoire de la Fondation de France/CerPhi, April 2015.

more than two times higher than that of American foundations (8.6%). The reason for this high ratio of expenditure in Europe is largely the fact that European philanthropists favour dynamic spending and fast social impact rather than the need for perpetuity. Changes to the legal and fiscal frameworks of many European countries also promote increasing number of European foundations and their high spending pattern. As a result, today, European foundations are characterized by their youth and dynamism, a sign that the philanthropic culture is continuing to make progress throughout Europe.

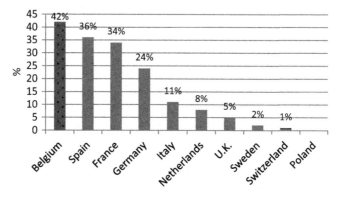

Figure 5.8.   Foundation vitality in 10 European countries (expenditure-to-assets ratio).
Note: No data available for Poland.
Source: Observatoire de la Fondation de France/CerPhi, April 2015.

Another characteristic of European foundations is the existence of very large *corporate foundations*. This is particularly the case in Germany. The operating model of German foundations is mainly through their corporate social responsibilities (CSRs) and grantmaking activities, which account for one-third of total foundation spending in Europe. In Italy, *savings bank foundations*, created in the 1990s, hold half of all Italian philanthropic assets, or 21% of the European total. Thus, one can say that European philanthropic capital is highly concentrated in German foundations and Italian *savings bank foundations*. At the other end of the spectrum, numerous foundations with very limited assets are also emerging everywhere in Europe, such as mainly through the creation of scientific cooperation, partnership, and university foundations, with public subsidies making up a quarter of their resources. Created more recently, the hospital foundation is also part of this public–private partnership trend in philanthropic organizations.

5.5 Favourable Fiscal Frame for European Philanthropy

It is remarkable that the states in all the countries studied offer tax advantages to private donors, which shows the governments' recognition of private initiative and individual expression of commitment to the common good. The British government introduced such a favourable fiscal system in the 1920s; Sweden, the last country to carry out tax breaks for charitable giving, began in 2012.

There are two types of *Tax incentives* in Europe:

(1) *Tax deduction*: the gift amount is deducted from taxable income. This is the mechanism used in the UK, Switzerland, Germany, Italy (although variants exist depending on the type of beneficiary), the Netherlands, Poland, and Sweden. The deduction has an upper limit that varies according to the country. The UK has a special tax deduction system through its Gift Aid and Payroll Giving mechanisms.

(2) *Tax reduction*: a tax credit is granted, the amount of which is proportional to the donation. This is the mechanism used in Belgium, France, and Spain. France has the highest rate (66% of the donation amount, compared with 45% in Belgium and 25% in Spain) and the highest upper limit (20% of taxable income, compared with 10% in Belgium and Spain).

It is difficult to compare these tax incentive mechanisms, especially where tax deduction and not reduction is involved. Nonetheless, these tax incentive mechanisms appear to have influenced the size of gifts made by individuals. In Switzerland, many cantons collect a church tax; in some cases, this is a percentage of the tax already owing, and sometimes an additional tax.

As most European governments encourage private generosity and giving through tax incentives, the governments recognize the need of structured and independent private initiatives and the role in civil society that the foundations sector can particularly play. Consequently, nowadays, the European governments see foundations, associations, federations, and other civil society organizations no longer as forming a kind of opposition force or a threat to them; instead they see them as part of an important and complementary sector for serving the public interest. Many foundations in Europe are taking responsibility for missions of public interest and social work, which the states cannot finance sufficiently or effectively over the long term.

In addition to the favourable fiscal environment for encouraging individual giving and contexts discussed above, internal changes in the foundation sector, starting with the foundation statute itself, also explain the recent boom in the number of foundations in several European countries.

For example, in France the introduction of new tax incentives for the foundations sector, namely, the creation of new legal forms — the endowment fund in 2008 — has resulted in the explosion in the number of foundations. This fund is characterized by its administrative flexibility with initially no start-up capital requirement, now amended to a low minimum threshold, and has led to the creation of more than 600 funds in just two years. Like endowment funds, *Treuhandstiftung* (fiduciary trusts) in Germany have experienced similar success. The creation of the fund does not require legal approval from the authorities, and this is often a first step in the philanthropic strategy of their founders, before the creation of a more traditional foundation. Similarly in Belgium, the already rapid growth of the sector has gained further momentum since 2002, owing to a new act governing the sector coming into force, giving legal recognition to foundations. In Spain, changes were introduced in two decisive years, 1994 and 2003, which modified the legal framework, and the measures have affected the further development of the sector.[11]

All in all, the philanthropic sector in Europe is explained largely through individual giving behaviour and the variety of foundation models existing in different European countries, as well as the ways in which philanthropic wealth is viewed. We have adopted the quantitative and qualitative methodology in analysing and measuring philanthropy in Europe from the perspectives of individual giving and foundations sector, and have discussed their characteristics and the tax environment for the growth of European philanthropy. We found that although the philanthropy sector of each country has its own specific features, owing to the introduction of new and varied legal frameworks, the lack of a requirement for an initial endowment, and expenditure incentives (Spanish foundations are required to spend 70% of their net annual resources) encouraged by their respective states, dynamism and vitality are European foundations' common characteristics. This dynamism is observed not only from the remarkable rise in the number of foundations, but also from the fact that those young and active European foundations define themselves primarily in terms of their actions rather than their assets.

---

[11] *Ibid.*

5.6 New Trends: Entrepreneurial Philanthropy Models

The big challenge that the European philanthropy sector is facing is how to increase the amount of capital in view of many small organizations' struggling to survive. For most European philanthropy organizations, in order to have an impact, the size of individual grants, loans, or equity may need to be in the millions of euros, thus giving the grantee the breathing space it needs. The merry-go-round of fund-raising is becoming more and more difficult for supporting the existence of many European foundations.

5.6.1 Driving Forces for Innovation in Philanthropy

In an environment where innovation is unquestioningly seen as obligatory, it is wise to take a more balanced approach. Currently, individual philanthropists have become more experienced and sophisticated; they recognize the need to address root causes of social issues, not merely to treat the symptoms. Given the scarcity of philanthropic resources, a new generation of philanthropists realized that philanthropy should be a form of *risk capital* to fund innovation and to prove their concepts, rather than continuously underwriting programmes that did not address underlying issues with a compelling theory of change. The call for innovation in philanthropy came especially from wealth managers, and private and public banks. Many American and European, including Swiss, wealth management firms and banks opened their offices in Asia and proposed new approaches to their High Net-Worth Clients.[12]

Innovation is usually described as the "specific tool of entrepreneurs ... by which they exploit change as an opportunity ..." More recently, it has been recognized that innovation also happens outside the business world — in the public and social sectors. "These sectors, too, have their entrepreneurs and intrapreneurs (change agents operating within existing organizations) who pursue innovative change across all stages of organizational life cycle — whether in new organizations, growing, or established ones."[13] It is widely accepted that innovation "doesn't happen

---

[12]From Switzerland, e.g. UBS, Crédit Suisse, Lombard et Odier.
[13]Rob and Tan *et al.* (2013, p. 28f).

automatically. It is driven by entrepreneurship — a potent mixture of vision, passion, energy, enthusiasm, insight, judgment and plain hard work which enables good ideas to become a reality."[14] A key question is also, which innovation is ethically positive and when can it turn out to be negative. Not every innovation is positive. To develop a cruel cluster bomb may be innovative, but it is not ethical.[15]

Contemporary economists interpret innovation as a cyclical process of "creative destruction," where old ideas, models and rules are destroyed while new ones are established in the search for profitability. It is generally accepted that *creating value* is the underlying purpose for innovation. Turning to philanthropy, Porter and Kramer in their 1999 *Harvard Business Review* article framed the new agenda for grantmaking foundations to be value creators, not passive intermediaries between individual donors and the non-profits or social enterprises that receive their funding.[16]

As it is widely believed that entrepreneurs and intrapreneurs are the primary agents of innovation, are there any entrepreneurs in philanthropy

Table 5.2.   Stimuli for innovation in philanthropy.

Frustration	Opportunity
• Discontent with the status quo in philanthropy. • Desire for greater sustained social impact. • Awareness that resources are used inefficiently. • A disconnect between business and philanthropy sectors. • Social issues are too complex for single interventions.	• Philanthropy is a globalizing sector. • Business entrepreneurs are creating wealth and are searching for models of philanthropy that have impact and connect with business approaches. • New generation of family-based philanthropists are reviewing traditional giving. • An increasing pool of professional talent seeking to volunteer. • Social entrepreneurship and hybrid organizational models are becoming mainstream, offering philanthropy beyond grantmaking.

Source: Rob and Tan *et al.* (201, p. 29).

---

[14] *Ibid.*
[15] See Bastos de Morais and Stückelberger (2014).
[16] Porter and Kramer (1999).

who stimulate the innovation journey in the sector? Rob and Tan view the stimuli for philanthropic innovation to be broadly themed around interconnected frustrations and opportunities as summarized in Table 5.2. The perception of philanthropy as a single and isolated issue of giving is no longer effective in today's world of complexity and integration. To create values and to achieve sustainable and beneficial impact, the philanthropy sector is called to be well-informed, to work collaboratively, and to be able to face the challenges presented by an increasingly globalized world.[17] A new word, "philanthro-capitalism," has come to exist lately to articulate philanthropy's challenge since the industrial revolution — to utilize business acumen in pursuit of the common good.

5.6.2 Venture Philanthropy

Venture philanthropy is a composite of the terms "Venture Capital" (off-exchange participation in risk-bearing ventures) and "Philanthropy" (private voluntary action with a charitable purpose); it takes concepts and techniques from venture capital finance and business management and applies them to achieving philanthropic goals.[18]

Philanthropic objectives can be attained not only through donations, but also, for example, through the issuing of loans or allowing for participation in the equity held by charitable organizations. There is no single global definition of venture philanthropy, and its definition has evolved over the years along with its practice.

Venture philanthropy was first developed in the US and was attributed to the American philanthropist John D. Rockefeller III, who described the need for a more "adventurous" approach to funding unpopular social causes. Thirty years later, *New Economy* philanthropists and academics foresaw the need for a reformed, energized, and more entrepreneurial culture of giving.[19] In the late 1990s, a rush of Silicon Valley's newly wealthy dot-com entrepreneurs became closely associated with the growing venture philanthropy movement, keen to apply commercial innovation to their grantmaking.

---

[17]Rob and Tan *et al.* (2013), *op. cit.*, p. 29.
[18]Weiss and Clark (2006).
[19]Rob and Tan *et al.* (2013), *op. cit.*, p. 39.

In Europe, venture philanthropy started during the early 2000s in the private equity and venture capital world of the UK, before seeping into the foundations sector across Europe. In 2004, the European Venture Philanthropy Association (EVPA) was established by individuals from the private equity industry who were looking for a model of giving that was more effective and aligned with their professional expertise as investment experts.[20] The EVPA was initially conceived as an informal network to encourage philanthropy in the private equity community, but it quickly gained support from more traditional grantmakers, professional service firms, and the private equity industry bodies. During the last decade, as governments and corporations began to inject significant capital into the field, venture philanthropy has spread into the foundations sector and social enterprises. With the growth in popularity and practice of social enterprise in Europe, and the fit between social entrepreneurs' demand and what venture philanthropy can offer, European venture philanthropy is now on the verge of growing from a noisy niche into an integral part of the broad philanthropic and socially responsible investment field.[21] By 2010 there were an estimated 48 venture philanthropy funds operating in 17 European countries. The EVPA's state-of-the-industry report in 2012 claimed that one billion Euros ($1.3 billion) had been invested by entrepreneurial philanthropy funds in Europe since beginning their operations. The figure combines financial support and estimated value of non-financial services donated as an integral part of the investment process.[22]

Venture philanthropy is believed to be growing in Europe, although it may not necessarily be under the banner of *venture philanthropy*. We have observed that many of the traditional foundations, corporate philanthropy, public policy initiatives, and impact investors are undertaking the programmes and projects consciously and unconsciously through applying venture philanthropy concepts into their actual operations. This implies that venture philanthropy may assume a different character in practical works. One of the differences that have already emerged is that venture philanthropy in Europe is much more diverse than it is in the US. Instead of relying on the traditional social democratic or welfare model of funding and operating social services, governments throughout Europe are now actively experimenting with models based on social enterprises and social

---

[20] *Ibid.*

[21] See the study Buckland *et al.* (2013).

[22] Rob and Tan *et al.* (2013), *op. cit.*, p. 39.

entrepreneurs. These new government approaches, combined with the growth of private venture philanthropy, may set the stage for significant changes in the European social landscape.

Nonetheless, the practice of venture philanthropy differs quite substantially from organization to organization. It has taken on *different forms in different countries*, each with its own unique set of laws, institutions, culture, and history, with a set of important characteristics distinguishing European venture philanthropy from other types of philanthropy and social investment, as identified as follows[23]:

- *High engagement*: the venture philanthropists are closely working with, and supervising the supported organizations' management.
- *Organizational capacity building*: by funding core operating costs rather than individual projects with the intention of building the operational capacity of the supported organizations.
- *Tailored financing*: through using a range of financing mechanisms, such as grants, debt, and equity, *tailored to the needs of the supported organization.*
- *Non-financial support*: providing value-added services such as strategic planning to strengthen management.
- *Involvement of networks*: through granting investees the access to networks of the venture philanthropists, which are often needed by the investees.
- *Multi-year support*: injecting the "seed" funds for a limited three to five years' period, then exiting when the supported organizations are financially or operationally sustainable.
- *Performance measurement*: the venture philanthropists emphasize *good business planning, measurable outcomes, achievement of milestones, and financial accountability and transparency* of the supported organizations.

This set of characteristics defines who are venture philanthropists in Europe regardless of *the financial tools used (grant, loan, or equity) or the type of organization financed (non-profit or for-profit)*. From this perspective, we can conclude that *social investors and pure grantmakers are both venture philanthropists in European terminology* in as much as they are highly engaged with their investees and they perceive the social impact to

---

[23]Buckland *et al.* (2013), *op. cit.*, p. 34.

be more important than the financial returns. These and similar activities across the European continent suggest that the future for European venture philanthropy is bright.

5.6.3   Social Entrepreneurship and Impact Investing

The steadily growing global phenomenon of social entrepreneurship has caused one of the most significant shifts in philanthropy over the last 50 years. Social entrepreneurs and their associated ventures are challenging the old paradigm whereby the grantmaking programmes of philanthropic organizations fund the project costs of charities through a reactive application process. The rise of social entrepreneurship coalesces with a new generation of philanthropists, many of whom are entrepreneurs wanting to connect their business acumen to their aspirations for charitable giving. They are younger than their predecessors, wanting to give while still developing their careers, many wanting to engage actively rather than give passively. They often question the effectiveness of more traditional charitable giving and speak more readily of "impact" and "outcome." Younger professionals, perhaps reflecting a broader re-evaluation of the nature of financial security, personal motivation, and responsibility to society, want to engage in charitable work with their volunteered skills.

This new generation of philanthropists asks 'how can we best fulfil our mission's objectives by responding to the innovations of social entrepreneurs?" In the new paradigm, the social entrepreneurship movement across America, Europe, and Asia comes at a time when the new generation of entrepreneurial philanthropists, often wealth creators and investors, look to give while professionally actively engaged.

Mission Investing (MI), also known as *Mission-Related Investing (MRI)*, for example, offers the possibility that an organization can pursue its mission while its assets remain invested. *The concept of incorporating the funding strategy in the investment policy therefore aims to reduce the dependence on financial returns.* As MI has developed, it has become an umbrella term that incorporates and overlaps with various value-based investment concepts, such as Socially Responsible Investing (SRI), or Impact Investing. These instruments, along with the empirical coverage of the practical implementation of MI are still in their formative stages.

As there is an unexpected large gap between the foundations' quest to becoming drivers and initiators of social innovation and actually realizing the concept and dealing with the process of social innovation, lately, it has become possible to critically question the role of foundations as social innovators. The functions of foundations in society and their role in the welfare state are also often questioned by the critics. It is suggested that the prerequisites for a foundation's strategy is that it should help to effectively initiate and support social innovations.

Under this context, the concept of "impact investing" has been widely spread in recent years after its first usage in 2008. The rise of "impact investing" has been a striking trend that has been well promoted globally. Pure philanthropy is a one-way flow of donation or capital that is always constrained. "The promise of impact investing is to create social value by investing in socially focused enterprises with sustainable business models, which, when successful, preserve capital and even offer a return on investment. Returns are reinvested in new ventures, and create a virtuous cycle of socially minded investment."[24] In 2009, the Global Impact Investing Network (GIIN) was launched by JP Morgan, the Rockefeller Foundation, and USAID, as the impact investing movement's advocacy. The same year, the Monitor Institute published its report on "investing with social and environmental impact." Over the next three years, several quantitative analyses followed, predicting the astronomic potential of the impact investing market. The 2011 report from JP Morgan and GIIN estimated $4 billion of potential impact investments for the following year and up to $1 trillion in the coming decade,[25] a figure supported by Credit Suisse in 2012.[26]

Until today, although entrepreneurial philanthropists have been limited in terms of using their capital for venture philanthropy, they are leveraging their resources through spreading their practices into other types of organizations where larger-scale capital exists to help venture philanthropists in their efforts to increase impact investing. This approach lends strength to venture philanthropy — it is a hybrid practice, with a great potential for cross-sector collaboration. Promisingly, we are already witnessing some of the effects of venture philanthropy's role as a catalyst in Europe. In the UK, where European venture philanthropy started, venture philanthropy has gone mainstream among foundations. Although many foundations do not use the term venture philanthropy, they have been increasingly supporting non-profit organizations and social enterprises

---

[24]See Rob and Tan (2013), *op. cit.*, p. 39.
[25]O'Donoho *et al.* (2010).
[26]Clark *et al.* (2012).

over multiple years. Among large foundations in Europe, many of them are corporate foundations that promote and engage in social responsibility programmes and projects. To a certain extent, this has become embedded in European corporate business culture. As a result, an increasing number of European corporate foundations have poured a large amount of funds into social-sector organizations. Leading corporate foundations such as BMW, Vodafone, and Shell are the major practitioners of venture philanthropy.[27] Another example is the social impact bond, a financial instrument pioneered in the UK that is used to fund programmes that save the government money. The investors of the first social impact bond in Peterborough prison included 17 individuals and foundations, not surprisingly including EVPA members such as Esmée Fairbairn Foundation that have previously invested in venture philanthropy funds.[28]

European governments are increasingly recognizing the potential of social enterprise and social investment and are starting to provide much-needed capital for intermediaries. UK's Big Society Capital, for example, is capitalized with up to £600 million from dormant accounts and high-street banks to develop "socially orientated investment organizations." The European Investment Fund is launching a fund of funds to invest in "social entrepreneurship funds." And the European Single Market Act, adopted in April 2011, includes the launch of the Social Business Initiative that notably makes access to funding for social businesses a priority.[29] From this perspective, we can say that the burgeoning number of social enterprises in Europe presents a growing opportunity for venture philanthropy investment.

In response to the growing social entrepreneurship movement, entrepreneurial expressions of philanthropy — along the whole spectrum from venture philanthropy to impact investing — are also developing in Asia. From our research, we found that entrepreneurial philanthropy is gaining in popularity in Asia, particularly among entrepreneurs and investment professionals. Today in Asia, especially in China, the term angel investing — "for helping small ventures grow to a stage where they can attract venture capital or private equity investment"[30] — has become a well-known concept in the philanthropy sector. In the commercial sector,

---

[27]Buckland *et al.* (2013), *op. cit.*, p. 39.
[28]*Ibid.*
[29]*Ibid.*
[30]Rob and Tan (2013), *op. cit.*, p. 39.

it appears that there are more angel investors who purchase equity in such ventures and work closely with the entrepreneurs in developing their businesses. This type of approach and practice is well suited to small social enterprises, which need business advice and capital expansion. We believe that with this trend, an increasing number of social enterprises will be able to largely benefit from wider use of impact angel investment; in return, it would lead to finding more impact investors and fuel the next stage of growth for both social enterprises and impact angel investing in Asia.

While these phenomena are broadly global, they are playing out with particular energy across Asia. *Avantage Ventures* estimates the potential demand for impact investing in Asia alone to be as much as $74 billion in the 10 years to 2020.[31] The entrepreneurial philanthropy models are catalyzing collaborations between the government and the philanthropic and social sectors. The number of funds and organizations devoted to this approach is increasing, as is the amount of money invested.

---

[31] Avantage Ventures (2011).

Chapter 6

Philanthropy in Switzerland: Dynamic and Developing*

6.1 A Rich Tradition

Switzerland enjoys a rich philanthropy tradition. One of its oldest registered foundations, called *Inselspital*, was founded in 1354 in Bern and it is still operating today. In 1835, the Zürich foundation law was passed; in 1907 the federal law followed suit, making Switzerland one of the most welcoming places for establishing a philanthropic foundation in Europe for most of the 20th century.[1] With more than 660 years' history of foundations, there were 13,075 foundations in Switzerland by 2015, among

---

*This chapter was originally published in Ling Ji and Christoph Stückelberger (2017). *Foundation Management, China Christian Series*. Geneva: Globethics Publications.

[1]"Summary: Lombard Odier Darier Hentsch (2010); A handbook for foundations in Switzerland offers Elisa Bortoluzzi Dubach, *Stiftungen. Der Leitfaden für Gesuchsteller*, Frauenfeld: Huber, 2007. A handbook for persons who want to create their own foundation or get an overview of foundation landscape: Sprecher, Thomas/Egger, Philipp/Schnurbein, Georg von, *Swiss Foundations Code 2015. Principles and Recommendations for the Establishment and Management of Grant-making Foundations*, Basel: Heling Lichtenhahn, 2016; VZ Ratgeber, *Spenden und Stiften*. Alles Wichtige zu Spenden, Vermächtnissen und Stiftungen. Mit Tipps zur Nachlassplanung und zum Steuern sparen, Zürich: VZ Vermögenszentrum 2008. Key information is also available on www.swissfoundations.ch and on the fundraising platform www.fundraiso.ch.

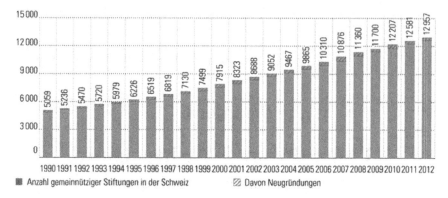

Figure 6.1.   Sustained growth in Swiss Foundations.

Source: Center for Philanthrophy Studies (CEPS)/NZZ-Infografik/tc. www.fundraiso.ch.

which 41.5% have been created since the year 2000 (see Figure 6.1).[2] The Canton of Basel-City has the highest number of foundations: 45.7 foundations per 10,000 inhabitants.[3]

Today, Switzerland is considered one of the most generous nations in Europe. Excluding church taxes, private giving recorded in the Swiss Confederation amounts to an estimated 1.2% of *annual disposable income*.[4] A Zurich-based spending-monitor agency revealed in 2008 that over two-thirds of households give regularly; while a typical Swiss-German donates a double amount of a Swiss-Romand (400–500 CHF versus 200 CHF) per year, both are around four times of their nearest neighbours — Germany and France, respectively. Giving by established foundations also appears healthy overall. The Swiss foundations' sector represents a large philanthropic resource with an estimated total asset of between 30 to 80 billion CHF.[5] The lack of exhaustive public data regarding Swiss foundations' assets and activities as well as the bank secrecy tradition make a more precise estimation hard to develop.

The Swiss foundations are mostly small, the sector is diverse, with numerous players, and is growing in number. By the end of 2015, there

---

[2] www.swissfoundations.ch.

[3] *Ibid.*

[4] Lombard Odier Darier Hentsch (2010).

[5] *Ibid.*

were 13,075 public-benefit foundations in existence in Switzerland, implying one foundation per 620 Swiss inhabitants. Among these, around 3,000 are operating foundations, and an estimated 3,000 are inactive, the remaining 6,000 or more are active grantmaking foundations.[6] Half of federally registered foundations give internationally. Most foundations stay small: at least 50% of foundations have assets of less than CHF 2 million, more than 36% started with assets of less than CHF 1 million, and 1/6 with assets of less than CHF 250,000. About 80% of the foundations in Switzerland have no employed staff.[7]

The *thematic focus* areas of Swiss foundations roughly are: 30–40% of foundations fund social issues, 25–30% fund art and culture, 13–20% fund education and science/research, and 6–9% fund health. There is no comprehensive and exact data available on the actual amount of annual giving to each focus area.

Apart from private giving and giving by established foundations, *Swiss companies* are also highly engaged in philanthropic activities. "More than three-quarters engage in corporate citizenship (giving and/or employee volunteering) — among larger companies, with more than 1,000 employees, this figure rises to 93%. Switzerland hosts a number of world business leaders in corporate philanthropy, including the efforts of many private banks. Moreover, corporate engagement looks set to expand further: based on the *Corporate Citizenship Survey*, 95% of companies intend to maintain or increase their Corporate Social Responsibility activity."[8]

6.2 Recent Developments

Numerous efforts have been made for developing the scale and impact of the philanthropy sector in Switzerland over the last 10 years or more. The establishments of proFonds and SwissFoundations mark the effort to consolidate and better structure the sector. Most indigenous Swiss foundations are members of proFonds and/or SwissFoundations implying that the scale of Swiss philanthropy sector is developing through well-organized platforms and networks. The following snapshots (see Table 6.1)

---

[6] *Ibid.*
[7] https://www.fundraiso.ch/stiftungen-schweiz/.
[8] Wehner (2009).

Table 6.1.   Recent developments of the Swiss philanthropy sector.

(A) Selected Information Sources and Tools in Switzerland

Identifying obstacles in a certain geography — Basel

FoundationFinder is a public interest association based in Basel founded in March 2009 with the goal of connecting those that are seeking grants and those that make grants. It is funded by the "Präsidialdepartement" of the canton Basel Stadt and by Gesellschaft für das Gute und Gemeinnützige, GGG Basel. FoundationFinder is also supported on content by the Centre for Philanthropy Studies (CEPS). Under www. foundationfinder.ch the public can access information about which funders are funding in their interest area. Information is based on publicly available sources and funders can log in and access/augment their specific information. Currently, the database has 800 funders in it, including those in Basel as well as members of SwissFoundations. *This type of database is a first step in allowing foundations and other types of funders to find cooperation partners.*

Identifying actors in a certain theme — Culture

The address database, *culturalpromotion.ch,* serves people active in the field of art and culture. It contains addresses of private and public cultural promotion (former *Handbuch der öfentlichen und privaten Kulturförderng in der Schweiz*) as well as addresses concerned with cultural networking and communication (e.g. stages, festivals, museums, press, and studios). The aim of *culturalpromotion.ch* is to create an interface between culture-promoting organizations and people involved in the cultural sector. Partners include *Schweizer Buchhändlerund Verleger-Verband* (SBVV), *Association Suisse des Diffuseurs, Editeurs et Libraires* (ASDEL), *Migros culture percentage, Kulturbüro Zurich, Pragma Music,* and *SwissFoundations.* Initially operated by the Swiss Cultural Office, the updating of the information is based on feedback from users. The directory today contains more than 5,000 addresses and 4,000 registered users. *This example shows that it is possible to capture a whole thematic sector in an online database.*

Providing a tool-kit — Cooperation among non-profits and corporations

The *Philias Humagora Online Partnership Guide* includes resources, tools, and best practices, available in both French and German, related to partnerships between corporations and non-profits organizations. *This type of tool-kit could be created on the topic of cooperation among foundations.*

(B) Selected Platforms for Knowledge Sharing and Peer Learning in Switzerland

Interfacing with peers on certain themes

SwissFoundations was initiated in 2001 to improve the image and the development possibilities of grantmaking foundations in Switzerland. SwissFoundations mobilizes in favour of transparency, professionalism, and the effective use of foundation means in the Swiss foundations field. Its 65 current members are all grantmaking

Table 6.1. (*Continued*)

foundations, providing support on various thematic domains, in Switzerland and abroad. SwissFoundations members interact in thematic working groups, including social, culture, education, research, innovation, and environment.

The thematic working groups are a strong platform for thematic networks that allow foundations to engage with each other on specific themes.

Interfacing with grantmaking and operating foundation peers

With a membership of 300 grantmaking and operating foundations, associations, and private members, *proFonds*, established 20 years ago, seeks to improve the conditions for philanthropic and social engagement with authorities and the political sphere, and to enable knowledge and information exchange among foundations. Cooperation among foundations and other types of funders was a key topic at the 2009 annual Swiss Foundation Day of *proFonds*.

ProFonds provides an opportunity for dialogue, learning, and action related to cross-sectoral cooperation.

Building cross-sectoral bridges around tactics and themes

Founded in 2006, the *Philanthropy Roundtables* in Zürich and Geneva connect select actors from the non-profit, business, and government sectors for knowledge exchange. Recent topics have included: poverty, media, and philanthropy, project selection, role of banks, taxes, and evaluation. These local discussion platforms are fertile grounds for promoting cooperation among foundations and other types of funders.

Building a foundation project directory

The *Stiftungsforum* is a lobbying, networking, and information exchange platform. It is building a foundation database that connects funders and projects to help enable coordination and collaboration.

This database is a great way to connect funders.

Engaging with peers on both theme and geography

The *Association de Geneve des Fondations Académiques* (AGFA), is an existing example of thematic funder cooperation. The members of AGFA are all focused on the academic sector, and from the Geneva area.

This network can be a platform for local/regional thematic cooperation.

Meeting with peers of similar interests

Wise — Philanthropy Advisors accompanies donors and their families in fulfilling their philanthropic aspirations. To enable peer learning, Wise brought together six families of entrepreneurs from all over Europe in 2009 to share their experiences in philanthropy. By bringing several generations to the table, everyone was able to create connections and exchange perspectives.

These types of venues enable philanthropists to form partnerships.

(*Continued*)

Table 6.1.   (*Continued*)

(C) Selected Jointly Funded Projects and Initiatives in Switzerland

An academic centre on philanthropy

The *Centre for Philanthropy Studies* (CEPS) at the University of Basel is an
interdisciplinary research and further education centre of the Swiss Foundation
System. CEPS was established in 2008 by SwissFoundations with initial funding
from AVINA Stiftung, Christoph Merlin Stiftung, Ernst Göhner Stiftung, Gebert Rüf
Stiftung, Gesellschaft für das Gute and Gemeinnützige GGG Basel, and Sophie und
Karl Binding Stiftung.

*This is an excellent example of funders coming together to create a lasting institution
that benefits the entire field.*

A fund for innovation

Funded by Gebert Rüf Stiftung, Ernst Göhner Stiftung, Opo Stiftung, and AVINA
Stiftung, *venture kick* aims for an early detection and promotion of promising business
ideas at Swiss universities and schools of higher education with the goal of doubling
the number of spin-offs by making startups attractive for professional investors.

*This is an innovative example of funders pooling resources to build a dynamic, stand-
alone thematic fund.*

A site for connecting young and old

A partnership of the Schweizerische Gemeinnützige Gesellschaft (SGG) and Pascale
Bruderer Wyss, President of the National Council, *Intergeneration* is an online
platform for posting and finding projects that encourage communication and
interaction between generations. Support came from several actors, including
infoclick.ch and Pro Senectute.

*This is a compelling example of the government partnering with the philanthropic sector
to achieve a political priority.*

A cross-sectoral support group for a critical cause

The ICRC and a group of selected Swiss companies and foundations have set up a
Corporate Support Group, establishing an innovative and long-term partnership. The
members of the Corporate Support Group have committed themselves to supporting
the ICRC's humanitarian work in the years ahead.

*This is an example of private corporate foundations coming together to support an
organization through funding and know-how.*

A public–private partnership around child protection

Announced in 2008, the *PPP-Programme National pour la Protection de l'Enfant* is a
nation-wide initiative around child protection, led by the Federal Social Insurance
Office and two private foundations: UBS Optimus Foundation and the Oak
Foundation.

*This is a groundbreaking example of a public–private partnership on a critical national
topic.*

Table 6.1. (*Continued*)

(D) Overview of Selected Umbrella Foundations in Switzerland

Established in 1972, the *Limmat Stiftung* aims to be a bridge between the rich and the poor, North and South, between donors and needy beneficiaries. The foundation is active both in Switzerland and abroad, endeavouring to stimulate, encourage, and support initiatives that serve the common good. It realizes its own projects and collaborates with individuals and/or institutions on other undertakings to achieve mutually desirable ends through 40–50 projects per year.

Since 2000 the *Ruetli Endowment* has been dedicated to supporting non-profit activity on behalf of its donors by evaluating requests, arranging payments to the applicants, and monitoring project developments in order to relieve the donor, if so desired, of the administrative tasks involved.

Stiftung Corymbo, founded in 2002, offers donors the opportunity to develop their charitable ideas without creating unnecessary administrative and organizational costs. The broadly defined statute of this foundation allows the different charitable funds to be grouped under one administrative umbrella in the areas of social services, health, education, environmental culture, arts, and sciences.

Three foundations supported by Credit Suisse (founded between 2000 and 2003) offer clients the opportunity to make a charitable commitment:
- *Accentus*: social/humanitarian issues, science and research, education, culture, environmental issues, and medicine;
- *Empiris*: research, science, and education;
- *Symphasis*: social welfare, preservation of nature, the environment, endangered species and wildlife, recreational and disabled sports, youth and seniors' sports, and culture.

Founded in 2006, *Stiftung Succursus* allows donors to realize their philanthropic goals without having to start their own foundation. Current fund topics of the foundation include: alternative energy, vacation, churches, financing for job seekers.

The goal of the *Swiss Philanthropy Foundation*, founded in 2006, is to promote the development of philanthropy by supporting organizations or projects of general interest, for example, in the fields of humanitarian aid, social or medical assistance, the protection of the environment, and culture. The foundation offers sheltered funds, and the ability to donate in Europe.

Fondation des Fondateurs, founded in 2007, is an independent, charitable umbrella foundation that offers private donors with small, medium-sized, and large volumes of funds the opportunity to make grants efficiently, cost-effectively, and professionally in support of causes and initiatives they favour. Current funds include the Lori and Karl Lutz Fund to remove obstacles in the way of girls' and women's education, and the *venture kick* Fund, described on the prior page.

(*Continued*)

Table 6.1.   (*Continued*)

Fondation Philanthropia is an umbrella foundation created in 2008 by the firm of
private bankers Lombard Odier Darier Hentsch & Cie to facilitate the philanthropic
engagement of its clients and help prevent unnecessary fragmentation in the field. It
offers a range of services from donor-advised funds to thematic giving allowing for
pooling of donor resources in the areas of scientific and medical research, culture and
education, social and humanitarian causes, and the environment and sustainable
development.

Source: Lombard Odier Darier Hentsch (2010, pp. 35–37).

give the details of recent developments in the current Swiss philanthropic
sector.

6.3 Legal Framework

The legal environment is particularly favourable for Swiss foundations.
The formation and registration of a foundation in Switzerland is quite
simple. It requires only a founding document that includes a defined purpose and it does not necessarily have to be for public benefit; then with
the founding document, it only needs to proceed to be listed on the
Register of Commerce of its domicile canton. Moreover, the required
capital for founding a foundation is only CHF 50,000 for foundations that
register at the federal level; and only CHF 10,000 for those that register at
the cantonal level.[9] The foundation types in Switzerland are various. Apart
from public-benefit foundations, it can also be established as an ecclesi-
astical foundation for church-related institutions (almost no new permitted), a staff welfare foundation (pension fund of a company), or a
corporate foundation — a foundation organized/established by a for-profit
enterprise for non-profit purposes, etc. All this ease and variety might be
a handicap as it contributes to the fragmentation of the sector and prevents
foundations from realizing their full potential.

Apart from the simple setting-up process and the variety of foundation types, Switzerland is also among the few countries in Europe that
allows, under certain conditions, *foundations to be repurposed after
having been established.* Only larger foundations are required to be

---

[9]*Ibid.*

audited annually. Data disclosure requirements are minimal. Under the current legislation, the Swiss authorities have limited powers of intervention and are perceived as reluctant to initiate sanctions against inactive foundations.[10]

The Swiss Foundation Code is currently considered the principle code of governance for non-profit and charitable organizations in Switzerland. This is a well-established, self-regulating instrument containing 29 recommendations, which has acquired an international reputation. The content is primarily addressed to donor foundations with the aim of offering assistance to foundation managers in their decision-making and in encouraging them to do a "good foundation management."[11] The Code provides a set of references, hierarchical structure, transparency, balance of powers, and efficiency. The Code aims to standardize governance of non-profit organizations in the form of typical behaviors of persons involved in foundations (especially, members of the foundation board). However, it aspires to be recognized as a guide to build trust rather than as a set of strict rules and rigid instructions. The Code, together with its commentary, operates in the field of law, but they must be considered as interdisciplinary instruments rather than strict legal documents. The Code has no character of law; it only has complementary reference force when the law is deficient.[12]

The Code is considered as a directive to the philanthropy sector on three essential points: first, *Recommendation 7* deals with the remuneration for members of foundation boards; second, *Recommendation 11* deals with the rules for adjudicating conflicts of interest; finally, *Recommendation 21* discusses investment strategies for foundation patrimony. This last theme enjoys an increasing supporting role with regard to new developments in the sector, such as venture philanthropy, specifically with mission-based investment or sustainable and socially responsible investments (SRI).[13] The Code is well on track to becoming a real Reference in practice and in scientific circles for various actors in not-for-profit and charitable organizations.

In view of the above, we can conclude that although the legal environment for the foundations sector in Switzerland is extremely generous with

---

[10] *Ibid.*

[11] Eckhardt *et al.* (2015, p. 35) (translation from French by the authors).

[12] *Ibid.*

[13] *Ibid.*

tax exemptions, encouraging start-ups with little capital (endowments), not requiring full audit for small foundations, allowing foundations to be repurposed, or inactive, and so on, the Swiss Foundation Code serves as an instrumental governance guide to the sector, enabling the sector to operate in a most professional and responsible manner, establishing the sector itself with a good reputation both at home and abroad.

6.4 Integrating Philanthropy with Wealth Management

Switzerland is the world's largest wealth management centre with 2 trillion USD assets under management at the end of 2014[14]; in other words, "25 percent of cross-border assets managed around the world are managed in Switzerland."[15] Approximately 50% of the assets under management come from abroad. Among these high net-worth (HNW) individuals/ families, some of them are Swiss natives; but many of them are originally from all over the world, people who are attracted by the stable and favourable political, economic, social, and legal systems of Switzerland, along with the Swiss tradition of banking secrecy. It is against this backdrop that the Swiss family offices and the wealth management of Swiss banks have not only come to exist, but have been flourishing.

6.4.1 Family Offices with Wealth Management

In Switzerland, a family office takes two major forms: a single-family office or a multi-family office. A single-family office normally is set up as a privately owned company that manages investments and trusts for a single family. A multi-family office serves at least two wealth families, ranging from a couple to a hundred wealth families or more; its client base is in all sizes. Some bigger family offices only accept clients with a minimum amount of wealth; and others serve all families able and willing to pay their fees. In Switzerland, by 2013 there were about 70 single-family offices and 400 multi-family offices;[16] it is expected that the number of

---

[14] www.deloitte.com, Press Release 1 February 2015.
[15] Swiss Bankers Association. http://www.swissbanking.org/en/financial-centre/key-figures/key-figures-2?set_language=en.
[16] Bar *et al.* (2012).

family offices would increase further given that the number of wealthy individuals and families are increasing steadily worldwide, and Switzerland is a reputed place for assets and wealth management.

A family office provides services and supports high net-worth individuals and wealthy families going far beyond traditional private banking services. It manages assets and the portfolios of their wealthy clients, giving legal and strategic advice, and eventually having the power of managing their clients' assets with the aim of risk avoidance and sustainable growth for their clients' wealth. One may find a family office anywhere in the world, particularly in Europe, Hong Kong, and Singapore. Other financial centres have also been involved in recent years in providing assets and wealth management services.

In Switzerland, a family office, in particular a multi-family office, offers a wide range of services to their clients for safeguarding and increasing their wealth. Their services range from wealth planning, administration, asset management, asset consolidation, asset performance monitoring, philanthropy advises, charity services, tax and legal services, trusteeship, risk management, caring for family members' education, and so on. These services are either offered from in-house professionals and experts; or by cooperating with dedicated external partners including Swiss private banks.

One of the core activities of a family office is to manage the wealth of HNW individuals/families in a profitable and risk mitigating manner. This explains why a family office normally spreads their HNW individuals/ families' assets over several different banks and jurisdictions for reducing counterparty risk. One of a family office's main works is to coordinate with those private banks where they have spread their clients' assets, and to keep track of these assets' performances with consolidated summaries in a monthly or quarterly report.

The existence and core activities of a large number of family offices in Switzerland have greatly facilitated the growth of wealth/asset management of Swiss private banks.

Swiss private banks normally manage HNW clients' assets/wealth via a discretionary mandate or act as investment advisors:

- *A discretionary mandate,* also called portfolio management, implies that the account-holder agrees beforehand with his/her bank on his/her own risk for allowing the bank to make all investment decisions on his/ her behalf.

- Acting as an *investment advisor* means that the bank only acts as the custodian of a client's assets; and the bank regularly makes investment suggestions to the client. It is the account-holder, or the family office, that makes the investment decisions and thus is primarily responsible for the performance and results on his/her own. The bank only performs as an investment advisor and a custodian of the client's assets.[17]

6.4.2 Integrating Philanthropic Services with Wealth Management

In recent years, many large family offices and leading private banks in Switzerland have started to include philanthropy and charity services into their business activities. We also see a growing number of not-for profit social enterprises whose main activities are providing charity or philanthropy advisory and impact investing consultancy services to wealthy families and individuals.

Given the trend that an increasing number of HNW individuals/ families are becoming more interested in philanthropy, they often have lacked the knowledge and expertise on how they can be engaged in the sector for achieving desired results and impact. Although today a nascent and growing pool of advisors exists in the philanthropy and charity sector, many HNW individuals and families still find that it is much simpler for them to just ask for information and guidance from their wealth managers. In order to serve their clients well, the Swiss family offices and private banks have naturally wanted to merge with philanthropic advisory services, which seem to become more and more important every year. As a result, philanthropy advisory services are being closely integrated with wealth management in the Swiss family offices and Swiss private banks. This phenomenon has been developed to an extent that there are a few family offices and banks having their own charitable foundations in which their clients can participate.

Not only is the Swiss family offices sector engaged in having their own charitable foundations, but a number of Swiss private banks are also expanding through an umbrella foundations structure. For example, *Fondation Philanthropia* is an umbrella foundation created by Lombard Odier & Co. — a renowned Swiss private bank — for its HNW clients

---

[17]Family Office Services Switzerland (FOSS), chapter on Wealth Management.

in 2008. *Fondation Philanthropia*[18] aims to reduce the administrative burden and costs associated with an independent foundation and to ensure donations are closely monitored and have an enduring impact as desired by its clients. *Fondation Philanthropia* also provides support for an area of activity or to specific projects, in its clients' own names or anonymously, or together with other donors, via participation in a thematic fund, or by setting up a personal fund. UBS bank's Philanthropy and Sustainable Investing Team has also been very active in providing philanthropy advisory services.

Taken as a whole, the practice of philanthropy in Switzerland has changed over the last two decades. Many HNW donors are no longer considering the philanthropy/charity act as a matter of simply signing a check. They now see philanthropy as a cause in which they want to engage in earlier in their lives and to focus on a specific project or cause with clear and measurable objectives. These new generation philanthropists also have new expectations such as involving their family members across generations into their philanthropic initiatives. Keeping this in mind, the services and activities of the Swiss family offices and the Swiss private banks have captured this demand through integrating philanthropy advisory services into wealth management, thus marking a special characteristic of Swiss philanthropy.

---

[18] http://www.fondationphilanthropia.org/.

Chapter 7

Philanthropy in China: An Update*

It has been widely accepted that earthquakes in China, notably in Wenchuan, Sichuan province, in 2008, and in Yunnan in 2014, have marked the recovery and acceleration of China's contemporary charity and philanthropy causes, which are internally driven by its citizen's common social consciousness and common social responsibility.

These have happened at a time marked by China's further opening to the outside world. On 29 September 2010, the famous American entrepreneurs and philanthropists Warren Buffett and Bill Gates came to Beijing to invite 50 Chinese tycoons to participate in a "charity dinner," causing a sensation. At this remarkable event, entrepreneurs from the two different cultures and traditions and their different perceptions on the concept of philanthropy led to exchanges, but also to forms of cooperation, which have had a wide range of effects on Chinese society and media.

Under the aforementioned circumstances, not surprisingly, the theme "China charity and philanthropy" has become a hot subject for current social science research, both domestically and internationally.

---

*This chapter was originally published in Ling Ji and Christoph Stückelberger (2017). *Foundation Management, China Christian Series*. Geneva: Globethics Publications.

7.1 Modern Challenges Shaping Chinese Philanthropy

7.1.1 Secular Characteristics of Chinese Philanthropy

As benevolence has been the cultural tradition of Chinese society since Confucius' time, the ancient rulers had frequently adopted benevolent policies for maintaining the sustainability of their rules. As early as the pre-Qin Dynasty, the ancient Chinese despotic empires often dealt with famines, poverty, healthcare, and other social issues. For instance, the granary system was established as a precaution against natural disasters and a stabilizer of food prices. The surplus grain was stored during harvest years and dispensed in case of catastrophes. Besides, the official institutions, such as poorhouses and sanatoriums, were built to provide accommodation and medical treatment for the homeless, the sick, and those who had no kith and kin.

Around the late Ming and the early Qing Dynasties, folk philanthropic organizations burgeoned owing to the prosperity of the commodity economy and the prevalence of morality books. These organizations were independently sponsored and administered by the populace, rather than the ancient governments. With abundant funds, philanthropic activities were conducted more frequently, and extensive strata including local gentries, merchants, and plebeians were engaged in aiding the elderly, orphans, widows, and others in need.

After the outbreak of the Opium War in 1840, China was turned into a semi-colonial society and underwent radical changes in the socio-economic, political, and cultural areas. In spite of the humiliation inflicted upon the Chinese nation, after the Opium War the Western colonists brought into China organized church activities, media, and the concept of social organizations even as the last Chinese Dynasty was faltering. The Democratic Revolution led by Dr. Sun Yat-sen witnessed a climax in philanthropy when overseas Chinese mobilized generous support to promising social organizations to overthrow the tumbling Qing Dynasty. Chinese philanthropy manifested new features during this period with the influence of Western values, which were largely spread via the missionaries, foreign newspapers, and progressive intellectuals who had returned from overseas.

Still, throughout this history, apart from the cultural characteristics discussed previously, Chinese philanthropy was largely secular, suggesting that the despotic empires in succession, and later on in the Republic state agencies as well as individuals, could get involved. These characteristics mark significant differences between the Western and Chinese philanthropy. While Western philanthropy is derived from religions, the Chinese philanthropic activities were conducted either by centrally governed disaster or poverty relief programmes, or by local gentries, merchants, and plebeians. This secular characteristic might explain the main reason why although Chinese philanthropy might not be short in numbers recorded; it was unable to parallel its counterpart in Europe either in magnitude or consistency.

7.1.2 Christian Characteristics of Chinese Philanthropy

Conversely, Christianity in China has had significant impact on the development of modern Chinese philanthropy. In the form of churches — and always linked with social, diaconal, and educative services — Christianity in China developed primarily in several phases:

(1) *In ancient times Christianity in China was alive in three periods*, in Nestorianism during Tang Dynasty (618–907 AD), with the Catholic Mission during Yuan Dynasty in the 13th century, mainly concentrated on the Mongolian area, and through the Jesuit Mission in the Ming Dynasty in the 16th century with the famous missionary Matteo Ricci.[1] Each time, Christian influence declined with the fall of the dynasty.

(2) During the *missionary period 1807–1949*, almost all Protestant denominational churches were present in China.[2] In addition, many free churches and Pietist movements like "Little Flock" emerged. Protestant missionaries set up 13 universities, and Catholic missionaries, 3 universities. They all are still functioning, now as state universities, among the top universities of the country. In addition to education, many hospitals, health, and social services had been built, financed by donations of Christians inside and outside China. Philanthropy was present in all these efforts.[3]

---

[1] Wang (2009).
[2] *Ibid.*, pp. 487–498. Also Tang (2001).
[3] A Study on Canton (in Chinese) (2005).

(3) *During the Maoist period 1949–1978*, Christianity was largely oppressed — 5,000 foreign missionaries had to leave the country in 1950, churches were destroyed or the buildings were used for other purposes. The Three-Self Patriotic Movement (TSPM), established in 1951, among others by Y. T. Wu, through the State Administration for Religious Affairs (SARA), emphasized the independence and autonomy of Christians from foreign funding, and supported development through "self-governance, self-support, and self-propagation" (hence, the "Three-Self" Movement). A key leader of these efforts was Bishop K. H. Ting, president of the post-denominational (united, Protestant) China Christian Council CCC, founded in 1980. He was also a long time, 1989–2008, vice-chairman of the Chinese People's Political Consultative Conference and member of the National People's Congress. He continued to emphasize the social responsibilities of Christians.[4]

(4) *Since the open-door policy 1978*, initiated by Deng Xiaoping by opening China for foreign businesses, the number of Christians in China has grown rapidly and, in parallel, social services and philanthropic activities have become very important. Bishop K. H. Ting and others founded the Amity Foundation[5] as early as 1985, as the development and charity organisation of the China Christian Council (CCC). It is the oldest Christian foundation for social services in modern China and one of the first Chinese NGOs established following China's Reform and Opening. It celebrated its 30th anniversary in Nanjing in 2015.

In China as in most countries around the world, religious believers donate more often than non-believers. A survey in China showed that 56% of Buddhists, 54% of Christians, 61% of Muslim, and 44% of Folk-religion believers regularly donate to charities. In terms of number of donations per year and total amount spent per person, Christians are on top.[6] In 2015, Amity Foundation alone raised donations of 150 million RMB, 76% coming from donations in Mainland China, 7% from

---

[4] See the collection of his speeches: Ting (2000, pp. 311–135).
[5] www.amityfoundation.org.
[6] Figures based on studies of Prof. Gao Shining, CASS Beijing, presented in Geneva/ Switzerland during an international conference, April 2014. Older study e.g. Lai (1992).

Hong Kong, and 17% from Europe and the US.[7] They support programmes in community development (rural and urban), health and disaster management, education, orphanages, and philanthropy training. In 2016, Amity Foundation established, as part of its internationalization strategy, a liaison office in Geneva, Switzerland, in cooperation with the Chinese-initiated Geneva Agape Foundation (GAF).[8]

7.2 Current Chinese Philanthropy and Foundations Landscape

7.2.1 Modern Chinese Philanthropy and the Social Reforms

With Deng Xiaoping's open-door policy since 1978 and China's fast economic growth from 1980s to early 2000s, a few social problems have become the major concerns in China's social and political life. One of the major issues is that the haze weather caused by air pollution, mainly due to the rapid expansion of heavy industries, has become a basic concern to the residents in Beijing and in many northern cities. These problems cannot be resolved by the government alone; they require a strong and responsible citizen's society. Under such social requests, China's modern philanthropy sector started to grow to become a significant part of China's social reforms. China's modern philanthropic society has been actively engaged in the advocacy of environmental protection, apart from participating in rural education, health, and cultural, art activities. From this perspective, China's modern philanthropy is playing a prominent role; it eases social contradictions, and at the same time promotes and leads social constructions, as well as combines morality and social ethics with new economic development. Thus, one can say that the modern Chinese philanthropy's positive social impact is enormous; it's one of the driving forces of China's on-going social reforms.

Chinese entrepreneurs, after fierce struggles in the business world, have accumulated enormous wealth under the current Chinese socialist market economy environment. Family enterprises are increasingly becoming the major force of China's economic development. Until July 31, 2014, out of 2,528 A-share listed companies, 1,485 were

---

[7] www.amityfoundation.org/eng/facts-figures.
[8] www.gafoundation.world.

private companies. Out of these listed private enterprises, 747 were family enterprises, accounting for 50.3% of listed companies.[9] In 2014, the number of Chinese multimillionaires has reached 109 million, while the billionaires are 67,000 in number.[10] From our observations, these wealthy entrepreneurs, especially the billionaires, with traditional Chinese cultural backgrounds, are more willing to devote their love and contributions to people of the same ethnic group, fellow citizens and citizens who are originally from the same villages or towns.

In short, China has long been a natural economic "acquaintance society," in which wealthy entrepreneurs, during their own life time, recognize that how they manage their wealth has become an unavoidable issue to deal with. They are deeply influenced by the ethical concept of "love has differential" (爱有差等), which is based on the patriarchal blood relationships in a traditional culture, which have formed their own philanthropic motivations that are different from those of Western entrepreneurs.

Being thankful is another important feature of modern Chinese entrepreneurs' philanthropic culture. There is not much controversy from the ancient until modern times on the fact that philanthropic ethics are rooted in compassion. But in actual philanthropic practices, Chinese entrepreneurs and foreign entrepreneurs are different. Chinese charitable activities emphasize gratitude, and pay more attention to brotherhood. The Chinese Confucian culture emphasizes "gratitude" and even advocates "to be grateful for a spring, for a helpful drip of water" (滴水之恩, 涌泉相报). Those who are ungrateful are severely condemned in the Chinese culture. Many entrepreneurs, even in the most difficult times of entrepreneurship, have received help from others. When they become successful and famous, they are bound to thank the society and others. In their view: (a) charitable giving is the expression of this gratitude; (b) being thankful is the basic ethical consciousness of human society; (c) charitable giving and gratitude are the two-way flow of human feelings. We conclude that gratitude is the second important factor in stimulating Chinese entrepreneurs' philanthropic enthusiasm apart from the kinship and community-oriented cultural philanthropic motivation.

Third, the Confucian concept of being an ethical profit-seeker is the spiritual motivation of Chinese entrepreneurial philanthropic ethics.

---

[9] "2014 家族企业传承主题论坛: 话传承心得, 谋长青之道," http://he.ce.cn/gd/201412/01.
[10] *Ibid.*

For thousands of years, the debate of being fair and ethical while being profitable as a significant theoretical proposition has been the focus of attention from various schools until today. In the relationship between morality and interests, Confucianism formed a complete theory of justice and benefit. In particular, Confucius' view of justice and benefit is appreciated and honoured by many Chinese entrepreneurs. Confucius believed that in the relationship between ethic and profit, "a gentleman is a righteous man; and "a small man is a profiteer," but he added: "richness and nobleness are people's desires, but [we] must get them with ethical ways." His descendants have summarized the meaning of this sentence as "a gentleman loves money, but to get it in an ethical way" (君子爱财, 取之有道). This has won universal praise among Chinese entrepreneurial groups, resulting in a far-reaching historical impact. In short, in Confucius' view of the difference between ethics and profits, ethics stands first; but ethics and profits under certain conditions can be unified.

In Chinese history, there is a title "Confucian entrepreneurs" (儒商). The so-called Confucian entrepreneur means, on the one hand, having the Confucian moral and intelligence; on the other hand, having businessmen's wealth and success. In other words, Confucian entrepreneurs achieve a good combination in the pursuit of material interests with morality. Such entrepreneurs are considered synonymous with philanthropists in the Chinese business culture. During these nearly 40 years of reform and opening up, the tide of the market economy has given birth to modern Chinese entrepreneurs' groups. They are not only the backbone of economic development, but also the backbone of the development of modern Chinese philanthropy in which Confucian ethics are the spiritual impetus in guiding their commitments to the development of China's modern philanthropic activities.

7.2.2 Social Engagement of Wealthy Chinese

Dynamic economic development, increasing social gaps, and environmental problems have been the main factors in stimulating the rapid growth of modern philanthropy in today's China. In the face of the widening gap between the rich and the poor, the role of charity as a third means of distribution in social life is being highlighted. Charity is an effective way to realize solidarity among the Chinese people, social fairness, and justice under China's new market economy. The evolution of Chinese philanthropy is manifested in the change from planning charity to civil philanthropy. Charitable giving nationally rose from US$6 billion in 2007 to US$13.8 billion in 2011. The earthquakes in China, notably in 2008 in Sichuan and 2014 in Yunnan, have led to huge outpourings of donations from the Chinese people across the whole nation, which are strong demonstrations of their massive civil engagement. According to *China Youth Daily*, by the end of April 2009, RMB 76.7 billion (then US$11.2 billion) had been donated to the Sichuan earthquake relief efforts. In the case of the Yunnan earthquake, the Red Cross Society of China had received a total RMB 72.5 million (US$11.7 million) five days after the earthquake.[11]

In recent years, some well-known domestic entrepreneurs have joined the ranks of charity. They have become the symbol of civil engagement and social development in China's modern philanthropy sector. "A boom in private foundations, led by the richest and most influential people in China such as the top ten Chinese billionaires and former Premier Zhu Rongji, has brought new blood to the philanthropy sector."[12]

Civil engagement can also be seen from the concept of social entre-preneurship, which came to China in 2004. With the growth of the philan-thropic sector, more "resources such as seed fund or patient capital are available for social enterprises in their early stages. The most successful social enterprises in China were launched and bloomed before the philan-thropy boom. Many foundations, including newly established private foundations, are reluctant to support grassroots activities because it seems to be too much work for a limited impact by small organizations."[13]

Starting from 2014, China's record for philanthropic giving has improved significantly. Jack Ma and his Alibaba co-founder Joe Tsai are at the top on the list of China's philanthropists through establishing a charitable foundation focused on pollution, the environment, and health, which is funded by 2% of Alibaba's equity. With the company's astonishing Initial Public Offering (IPO), it puts the charity's fund in the billions of dollars.[14] During 2015, several charity foundations were set up by a few of the second-generation rich and well-known art and media personalities. Among these, Lao Niu Brother & Sister Foundation

---

[11]Russell and Zhang (2015).

[12]Li (2013).

[13]*Ibid.*

[14]Russell (2015), *op. cit.*

(老牛兄妹基金会 — also referred to as the Chinese Edition of the Rockefeller Foundation) is one of the most well known. China's famous media figure and philanthropist ambassador Yang Lan (杨澜)'s Sunshine Culture Foundation (阳光文化基金会) is also well reported in China's philanthropy media. "The Chinese society is at a transition point, and philanthropy has a unique role to play to create and accumulate social wealth. Philanthropic leaders need to take the initiative and modernize philanthropy culture by motivating and empowering the majority of Chinese to become part of the solution. Philanthropy in China needs to shift from a rich man's club to civil engagement, and to move beyond mercy money to promoting positive social change."[15]

7.2.3 Corporate Social Responsibility and Entrepreneurs' Philanthropy

On the international stage, the development of China's charity can improve Chinese enterprise standards in terms of social responsibility as the major influential transnational companies have taken socially conscious programmes and promoted philanthropic ideas. China's philanthropy has been definitely contributing to the healthy development of global social innovations. In most cases, and not only for Chinese companies, *corporate social responsibility (CSR) is interpreted as corporate philanthropy.* "The core characteristic of CSR is not about how to spend money but, rather, about how to make money in a sustainable and responsible manner. The days when organizations focused solely on becoming the country's most profitable are long gone. Today, leading Chinese companies seek to become some of the world's most reputable and pre-eminent brands. They view CSR as a critical part of their transformation. During face-to-face interviews carried out by the United Nations Global Compact, some Chinese business leaders echoed this sentiment, saying that being on the *Fortune* 500 list is not sufficient for maintaining competitiveness in global markets and that their companies must evolve, particularly in the area of CSR, if they are to achieve their lofty goals."[16] A number of companies have started to view CSR as something more than just making donations, publicity opportunities, and/or risk control.

---

[15]Li (2013), *op. cit.*
[16]Liu (2015).

These firms are beginning to understand CSR's role and value in achieving a "triple win" for business, society, and the environment.

Apart from various institutional pressures (government, industry, communities, media, NGOs, and unions), the other main driving forces for China's CSR development are: to ease national employment pressures; to save China from environmental catastrophe; and to adapt to Chinese companies' global expansion. A growing number of Chinese companies are expanding their business operations into overseas markets. As part of this process, they are being exposed to more developed approaches to CSR. In many cases, they are also under growing pressure from global business partners and other stakeholders to improve their CSR performance. "CSR is widely seen as the way to help companies operate responsibly and in an environmentally sustainable way. Positive performance in these areas in return for consumer and local community support, or a "social licence," is viewed as an informal contract between companies and local stakeholders."[17]

Figures 7.1 and 7.2 are illustrations of the recent online surveys co-conducted by CSR Asia and the Embassy of Sweden in Beijing. We have noted that in some regions, local governments have established specific targets and standards for energy saving and reduction of emissions. Companies that fail to comply have had their operations suspended. Against this backdrop, many influential Chinese multinational companies have been diversifying their business activities into the green energy sector, which is not only viewed as a part of their CSR approach, but also as a part of their strategic development. With the growing presence and influence of Chinese companies abroad, some leading State-Owned Enterprises (SOEs) — including Sinosteel, Sinopec, China Minmetals, and China National Petroleum Corporation (CNPC) — have begun to publicly disclose their social investment and impact in Africa through their CSR reports with dedicated efforts to address and showcase sustainability activities in the region.

According to our observation and confirmed by Liu Meng, "the concept of CSR has been well supported by the Chinese government. The turning point came on 1 January 2006, when the Chinese corporate law was revised to formally include the concept of CSR in legislation. In the same year, the State Grid Corporation of China issued the first-ever CSR

---

[17] *Ibid.*

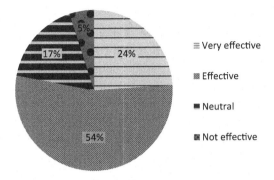

Figure 7.1.   To what extent has CSR been effective in addressing social/environmental issues in China.

Source: CSR Asia & Embassy of Sweden (2015).

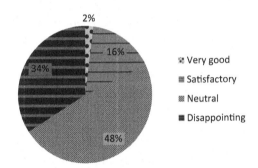

Figure 7.2.   Current state of satisfaction with level of CSR development.

Source: CSR Asia & Embassy of Sweden (2015).

report by a Chinese State-Owned Enterprise (SOE)".[18] Nonetheless, China wanted to create its own CSR definition and guidelines that embedded its unique economic situation and business culture. In 2008, the State-Owned Assets Supervision and Administration Commission of the State Council (SASAC) issued an important policy directive on *Guidelines to the State-Owned Enterprises Directly Managed under the Central Government on Fulfilling Corporate Social Responsibilities.* "In 2009, during a meeting with the leaders of (SOEs), SASAC mandated that all

---

[18] *Ibid.*

SOEs under their management set up a CSR mechanism within their governance structures. SASAC further mandated that all SOEs under its supervision publish their first CSR report by the end of 2012 if they have not done so already. This policy and the subsequent momentum led to the release of more than 1,600 Chinese sustainability reports. Half of these reports were from SOEs or listed companies and represented a significant jump compared to the 22 CSR reports from China between 1999 and 2005."[19] *SynTao*, a Chinese Beijing-based consultancy firm specialized in CSR, offers an online directory with 6,000 CSR Reports,[20] searchable in Chinese. CSR stands here for Corporate Sustainability Reports as well as for Corporate Social Responsibility. In February 2016, Globethics.net Foundation, based in Geneva in cooperation with China's *SynTao*, released the online directory of 6,000 sustainability reports fully searchable in English.[21]

"Today, SASAC is exploring how to build an internal system to evaluate the CSR performance of its member companies. This includes, for example, how a company's impact on the environment will affect its top leaders' remuneration, and setting incentives to serve as a next step to enhance corporate sustainability and global competitiveness."[22]

The following expectations regarding the future development of CSR in China emerged from our research:

- The government is expected to strengthen enforcement of legislation and regulations, especially in the areas of environmental pollution controls, working conditions, and anti-corruption.
- Traditional media is expected to expand its CSR reporting scope beyond its current emphasis on corporate philanthropy.
- More engagement and collaborative initiatives are expected to be developed within and among different stakeholder groups, including strategic long-term partnerships between government, businesses, and civil society.
- Large international companies are expected to work more closely with their Chinese partners on CSR-related issues, providing broad support

---

[19] *Ibid.*

[20] www.syntao.com.

[21] Syntao, http://www.globethics.net/library/collections/chinese-csr-reports.

[22] Liu (2015), *op. cit.*

through sharing professional knowledge and best practices with the aim of developing mutually beneficial long-term business relationships.

- There is growing consideration of how CSR can be more effectively implemented through its incorporation into the management structures and the development of action plans with concrete targets and performance indicators.

In sum, like many of their Western counterparts, Chinese companies faced a variety of governmental, societal, and market pressures that prompted their CSR journey. However, perhaps more than their competitors, many Chinese companies see their futures as inextricably linked to their CSR performance and have begun viewing it as a potential competitive edge. From this perspective, we believe that China will become a leader, not a follower, in the CSR domain. To date, there are more than 400 Chinese companies that are members of United Nations Global Compact; this number is predicted to increase according to our forecast.

7.3 New Developments

7.3.1 Boom in Foundations

The Ministry of Civil Affairs of China classifies Chinese civil organizations into three types: social organizations, private non-enterprise units, and foundations. According to China's official definition, social organizations are "non-profit civil organizations voluntarily established by Chinese citizens for the realization of a common desire of the membership in accordance with their articles of association."[23]

Before 1980s, there were no modern philanthropic organizations in China. Starting from early 1980s, some charitable and philanthropic organizations emerged, but these efforts were mainly led by the government. Since 2004, with the new *Regulations on the Administration of Foundations* coming into effect, the private sector can finally participate in the development of the philanthropy and charity field. The promulgation of *Regulations on the Administration of Foundations* was thus a milestone in that a new sort of foundation — private fund-raising foundations — was introduced, which was significant given the fact that

---

[23]Ministry of Civil Affairs of China, (1998), Art. 2.

most foundations at that time were sponsored by the government. There is a very strict definition of foundations under China's 2004 *Regulation on the Administration of Foundations*. Under this law, there are two major categories of foundations: public fund-raising foundations and private fund-raising foundations (referring to those not permitted to raise funds from the public).[24]

Due to sponsorship from the government, public fund-raising foundations established prior to 2004 were generally endowed with more initial capital, in fact double that of private fund-raising foundations. But the situation was reversed for those set up after 2004, when more enterprises engaged in philanthropy via corporate foundations with a large amount of initial capital. Thus, the *Regulation* of 2004 encouraged individuals and enterprises to enter the philanthropic sector by liberalizing the flow of private capital through raising private funds. Still, during this period, the restrictions on activities and the issue of tax exemption were some of the challenges facing Chinese foundations. Another challenging area for Chinese foundations was the running of their own programmes, and meeting transparency standards.

It was against this backdrop, initiated by 35 influential Chinese foundations, that the China Foundation Center (CFC), a non-profit supporting organization, was established in 2010. According to a China Central Television (CCTV) news report, CFC is hoping to keep up pressure on charitable foundations through the *China Foundation Transparency Index*, which ranks Chinese foundations against a checklist of 60 "transparency" indicators based on publicly disclosed information about the foundations' activities, finance, and governance. The CFC mission is to bring *transparency and trust* to philanthropic markets through access to the highest quality data, news, and analytics to enhance the social impact of philanthropy.

Figure 7.3 shows that since 2009 the number of charitable organizations and the amount of donations have increased year by year; the types of charitable/social organizations have been varied as well, such as grassroots organizations, private non-enterprise units, and corporate foundations. With a mass of social organizations coming into being since 2009, the numbers of foundations have seen rapid growth, particularly in private

---

[24]Ministry of Civil Affairs of China, (2004), Art. 3.

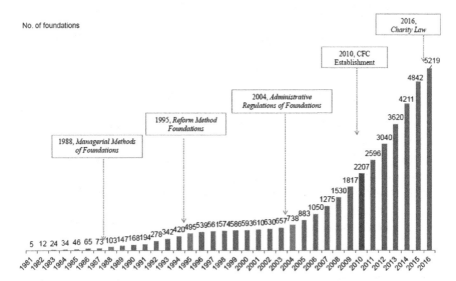

Figure 7.3.   History of Chinese Foundations.

Source: China Foundation Center, FTI, 31 October 2016.

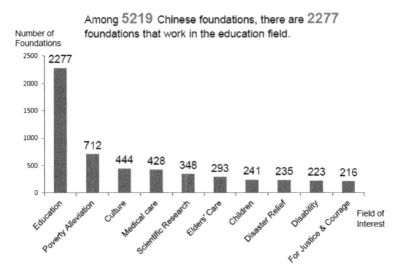

Figure 7.4.   Sectorial distribution of the Chinese foundations: Top 10 fields of interest.

Source: China Foundation Center, FTI, 31 October 2016.

fund-raising foundations, which count for around two-thirds of the total number of foundations in the country. By October 2016, the number of Chinese foundations reached 5,219 in total.

The ranges of activities of these foundations are mainly in education, environment, science and technology, disaster relief, and cultural exchange. While a strong emphasis in Chinese philanthropy is placed on supporting the poor, by far, the biggest recipient of philanthropy donations is the education sector, with the environment and healthcare the next two largest sectors. Figure 7.4 indicates the sectorial distribution of the Chinese foundations; among 5,219 Chinese foundations, 2,277 of them work in the education field, followed by the poverty alleviation, culture, and medical care fields.

In spite of the recent development, it is noticeable that public fund-raising foundations, no matter when they were established, enjoy more advantages in charitable fund-raising as they are exposed to a larger base of potential benefactors in terms of their experience, reputation, and governance structure. The public tends to believe that the foundations with a longer history and government sponsorship seem to be more competent and trustworthy.

7.3.2 Putting Philanthropy on the Map

In the 21st century, China's GDP has been ranked the second in the world after the US, but the Charities Aid Foundation's 2014 World Giving Index shows that the Chinese mainland only ranked 128th among the list of 135 countries and regions; whereas the US and Myanmar topped the list.[25] This is disproportionate to China's position and image in the international arena, particularly in view of the fact that China is home to the second-highest number of billionaires, behind only the US.

One of the principal reasons for the lack of charitable giving in China compared to the US and other European countries is the issue of trust and transparency. The public is apprehensive about the funds being misused, and this lack of trust is supported by the fact that less than a third of registered charities met transparency and disclosure standards. Angered by scandals involving the China Red Cross and other large public

---

[25]"环球一周民意调查话题榜," 《环球时报》, 2014年11月28日.

foundations, there is concern that donations would be misused or flow back to the government.

The lack of regulation is also another factor that hampers philanthropic causes in China. By law, charities are required to have significant start-up funds, and in practice many were not exempt from tax, and neither were there clear rules about how funds were to be used, their taxability, or any conflicts of interest. This improved substantially, as we have seen previously, with the new Charity Law of 2016.

Third, the charity sector was firmly a part of the State, and currently is still in its infancy. The powerful and strong government that dominates the public sphere has been one of reasons for the lack of civil society in China. The fourth, the desire of many of China's wealthy to keep a low profile, not drawing attention to their riches, also keeps China's significant philanthropic gestures at a minimum.

There is a huge potential that philanthropy can and has to help solve the social contradiction of the widening gap between the rich and the poor, to realize social harmony. The historical experience of the US and European countries show that entrepreneurs are one key force for the development of philanthropy. Through charitable and entrepreneurial philanthropic activities, they can contribute significantly to easing social problems and promoting the development of national and social equalities.

To overcome the obstacles faced by Chinese philanthropy, especially by the companies whose main domain is social welfare, China needs to not only actively promote social advocacies and to change social concepts, but also to adjust the relevant systems and policies that link closely to social welfare enterprises, as the Chinese masses generally do not believe that charity can be combined with business, which can be accomplished through social innovations.

Since 2013, the Chinese government has begun to actively implement social reform. The government has announced eliminating the double management systems on charitable organizations, that is, it no longer requires these organizations to register under the competent unit system of the State. The State Council also decided to purchase services provided by some social organizations, which is interpreted as a meaningful public policy transformation. In the philanthropic field, many organizations started to pay attention to promote their own reforms and to explore innovations of various aspects. It's obvious that the benign interactions between the government and the society will make China's philanthropy contribute much more to the overall social reforms in China.

From our observation, in today's China, the general trend indicates the close integration of philanthropy and social system reform. Setting up the modern social organizations system is one of the most significant parts of social system reform. At present, Chinese philanthropy is stepping into a new stage in pushing the social system reform forward, and in propelling social government organizations to be more open and transparent.

Today, as the Chinese entrepreneurs face a great development period of philanthropy, the state is in the process of introducing laws and policies on the governance of philanthropy, supporting and standardizing the charitable activities of entrepreneurs. The establishment of the China Foundation Center (CFC) means the greater promotion of transparency and accountability among the Chinese foundations. From this indication, we can see that the Chinese government, along with its non-profit organizations (NPO) sector, aims at putting philanthropy on the map through increasing the sector's transparency and accountability.

7.3.3 Venture Philanthropy and Social Entrepreneurship

Nowadays, Chinese philanthropic organizations are relatively small; nonetheless, *impact investing* or venture philanthropy has started to develop in today's China although it is still at an early development stage. In fact, there is a recent trend among Chinese philanthropists wanting to learn the different forms and tools from their European and American counterparts through the innovative process of adoption, adaptation, and refinement for conducting their philanthropic activities in China. One of the newest concepts that has caught the attention of the Chinese philanthropists as well as other Asian countries' philanthropists is: Venture Philanthropy.

With the modern practice of entrepreneurial philanthropy being such a recent phenomenon, it is perhaps surprising how much activity is apparent across Asia today, given that philanthropy in general is only just emerging in the region. There is no accurate data on the number of venture philanthropists and impact investing funds active in Asia, although the Asia Centre for Social Entrepreneurship and Philanthropy's exercise in 2011 estimated 58 funds. The Asian Venture Philanthropy Network (AVPN) launched in 2012 now has 123 members. Of these, 42 are categorized as "Practising Members" (that is they qualify by virtue of 'practising either venture philanthropy or impact investing' in Asia.[26] Since not all funds will become members of AVPN, this figure is a very conservative estimate of indigenous entrepreneurial philanthropy.

Philanthropy is rapidly developing throughout most of Asia, driven by an unprecedented growth in personal wealth. For the first time, Asia Pacific is home to the largest population of high net-worth individuals (HNWIs) of any regions; resulting from a 1.6% expansion from 2010 to 3.37 million in 2011 (Europe has 3.2 million, North America, 3.35 million, with Latin America, Africa, and the Middle East sharing the remaining 1.1 million). Total HNWI wealth held by Asians in 2011 stood at US$10.7 trillion.[27]

Angel-type investment is another entrepreneurial expression of philanthropy that is favoured by today's modern Chinese philanthropists. Angel investing, like all engaged models, is more than funding a good idea or a promising organization. It involves a partnership of mutual responsibility and respect, and a clear alignment of interests. This angel philanthropy provides a continuum of financing model for non-profits and social enterprises at all stages of their lifecycle. Impact angel investors complement the activities of enterprise philanthropists in helping social businesses in their early stages of development. Social entrepreneurship and its accompanying organizational forms — entrepreneurial non-profits, social enterprises, and businesses that offer low-cost goods and services to the poor — all offer new opportunities for creating social value in ways that differ from traditional charitable approaches.

In conclusion, social innovation, in the Chinese context, is reflected in three areas: government innovation, communist party innovation, and social innovation. Although the first two are the main battlefields that need a certain amount of time, the Chinese government and communist party have taken numerous legal and regulative measures in facilitating the growth of the charity/philanthropy sector. Chinese social innovation is promising along with the philanthropy and charity field as the best breakthrough point. For Chinese social innovators and foresighted philanthropists, introducing business mentality and corporate operating models into philanthropic organizations can effectively expand their scale and systematic development, and turn those organizations into attractive partners,

---

[26] See Rob and Tan (2013), *op. cit.*, p. 40.
[27] *Ibid.*, p. 21.

able to leverage government and all kinds of social resources. As a matter of fact, Chinese philanthropists are currently in the process of exploring different forms of philanthropic initiatives just like the European and American philanthropists, among which, combining with social innovation concepts, "impact investing" and "venture philanthropy" are fully in the process of contributing to putting Chinese philanthropy on the map.

Chapter 8

Foundations Management:
Governance, Funding, Communication[*]

Do good and do it well. This sentence shows that philanthropy needs a good heart, good intentions, and vision, but also good management. A good number of high net-worth individuals (HNWI) discover, after a long life of wealth accumulation and their initiation into philanthropic activities, that spending money is even more difficult than earning money. This means: in order to have long-term impact through philanthropy, professional management of programmes is needed as in professional activities in business, education, or public administration. This chapter therefore aims at giving inputs and an orientation on management tasks and instruments in philanthropy, more precisely on foundation management. The chapter is directly addressed to you as readers, as persons who plan to establish a foundation, or get involved in foundation and project management.

Despite the lack of a common definition of "foundation" across Europe, the *European Foundation Centre (EFC)*, in consultation with its members, was able to develop in 2001 a provisional definition of "public benefit foundations" that served as a basis for the one used in this book. The definition of the EFC is as follows: Public benefit foundations are independent, separately constituted non-profit bodies with their own established and reliable sources of income, usually but not exclusively

---

[*]This chapter was originally published in Ling Ji and Christoph Stückelberger (2017). *Foundation Management, China Christian Series*. Geneva: Globethics Publications.

from an endowment, and with their own governing board. They distribute their financial resources for educational, cultural, religious, social, or other public benefit purposes, either by supporting associations, charities, educational institutions, or individuals; or by operating their own programmes.[1]

In May 2014, DAFNE organized a conversation among its members to discuss and validate the EFC definition. At that meeting, DAFNE members unanimously agreed that the DAFNE/EFC definition was sufficient to allow "public benefit foundations" to be counted in their countries. The organization *Swiss Foundations* is a partner member of EFC. It also adopts the above definition. In this chapter, unless otherwise specified, "foundation" refers to a "public benefit foundation," and "foundation management" refers to "public benefit foundation management."

8.1　Vision, Mission, and Values

8.1.1　Questions on *What* Do I Want?

Whether you are just starting out or running a long-standing foundation, philanthropy is iterative. It is natural and essential to query, review, or form the basis on which the foundation is run. This basis is: what are your or your foundation's vision, values, and principles? These visions, values, and principles are mostly based on philanthropic aspiration. Previously, it has been mentioned that the origin of the word "philanthropy" in Greek is *philanthropia*, which literally means "love for human beings." Beyond the simple act of being charitable, modern philanthropy implies a strong desire to understand and resolve issues/problems, and a strong personal commitment to imparting positive change. Keeping this in mind, you/your foundation must be enabled to:

- "adapt your philanthropy to a changing environment
- improve your operations to optimize your impact
- stay true to your initial vision."[2]

---

[1] http://dafne-online.eu/wp-content/uploads/2016/10/PBF-Report-2016-9-30-16.pdf, 3.
[2] UBS Philanthropy Compass, Zurich 2014, 34f. Free download: www.ubs.com/philanthropy.

"What is a *vision?* For a philanthropist or a funder of a public benefit foundation, a vision describes what you want the world to look like. It is both idealistic and long term, and serves as an inspiration and motivation for driving."[3] Forming your vision is the most crucial step for your philanthropy and your foundation, because it will lay the foundation for all further activities. Therefore, you as founder must take your time and ask as many questions as possible, of yourself as well as of others when you prepare what kind of philanthropy you aim at doing.

The first question could be: *What do I want to achieve?* In almost every field of human activity, faced with such a wide range of possibilities, thoughtful and focused giving and activities can make life better.

You may already have a detailed vision of what you want to achieve through your philanthropy. Your desire to engage may be based on a particular experience, on an affinity to a country or a specific community or it may stem from your wish to continue to use your professional expertise in a social context. All this will help you find a starting point and narrow down what you want to achieve.

Your vision will be of central importance to your philanthropic journey and is the basis, *the foundation, of your foundation.* "The best vision statements make a bold, clear-sighted statement about how things should be, while leaving room for innovation and evolution in how to achieve it."[4]

A mission statement is a concise description of an enduring purpose. Your mission statement will be crucial for explaining and sharing with others what you are doing. "It is the written manifestation of your intentions and enables you to check constantly if you are staying true to your course."

After having formed your vision, you should look into the following elements for the mission statement:

- *Aspirational*: describing how things should be, rather than as they are.
- *Focused*: setting out the "what," "where," and "whom" that will anchor efforts.
- *Concise*: summing up intentions in a crisp and understandable way.
- *Memorable*: catching the attention of potential partners, and inspiring their actions.[5]

---

[3] *Ibid.*, p. 21.
[4] *Ibid.*, p. 24.
[5] *Ibid.*

The overall mission statement you set for yourself or your foundation will be closely related to your vision. The main difference between the two is that the mission is more concrete, possibly with a set time frame and an indication of how you will act. For example, the Amity Foundation's vision is: abundant lives, more justice, and a better world (让生命更丰盛, 让社会更公正, 让世界更美好). While its mission statement is: Abiding by principles of mutual respect and interfaith harmony, Amity builds friendship with people at home and abroad. Through the promotion of holistic development and public welfare, Amity serves society, benefits the people, and contributes to world peace (在信仰互相尊重的原则下共同献策出力, 开展同海内外的友好交往, 发展我国的社会公益事业, 促进社会发展, 服务社会、 造福人群, 维护世界和平).

"Knowing what your motives and resources are as well as where you would like to focus them is all you need to start drafting your first mission statement. It will remain a working document for a long time; indeed, it will drive the entire planning of your philanthropy. So don't rush to it, and keep in mind that a vision statement is never fundamentally right or wrong."[6] It represents your choice!

Values are benchmarks of orientation of what is right and wrong and what "ought" to be. Equality (e.g. Equal rights for all), Justice (e.g. fair treatment and fair distribution), Freedom (e.g. the power to decide and implement goals), Responsibility, Peace, or Empowerment are such fundamental values. They are connected to each other. Each of these values, if isolated and maximized, turns into a non-value. For example, freedom maximized turns to a Wild-West anarchical type of society where the strongest wins and oppresses the others. But freedom balanced with equality and fairness sees the limit of one's freedom in the freedom of the other and therefore is community-oriented.

Values influence attitudes, behaviour, decisions, and actions to a great extent. Priorities in decisions are an expression of priorities of values.[7] As values are general benchmarks for individuals and communities/ institutions, virtues are benchmarks for personal behaviour: respect, integrity, honesty, modesty, etc. Virtues influence to a great extent behaviour just as vices, the negative side of virtues, also do.[8]

---

[6] *Ibid.*
[7] More on values: Stückelberger *et al.* (2016), Stückelberger (2016a).
[8] 26 Values and Virtues are explained in a intercultural context in: Stückelberger *et al.* (2016), *op. cit.*

Figure 8.1.   Forming your vision, mission, and values.

For a foundation, clearly defining its values permits it to form various actions. Values allow an organization to launch a common approach. Without values being clearly identified, a foundation/organization cannot move forward. How can it develop its image, its reputation, and its identity without values? Values represent the framework of actions for an organization.

The diagram (Figure 8.1) above indicates a process of self-reflection by drawing on your motivations and experiences, and your skills and resources, to decide what issue you want to focus on, whom you want to help, and where you want to act. "This process is one that can be very personal, often evoking difficult memories or experiences. It is one that also takes time in order to gain clarity about your motives and expectations, as well as to acquire the knowledge that allows you to make tangible, informed, decisions."[9]

"**What** issue will you focus on?

- Make progress on a **health** issue
- Address **environmental** concerns
- Promote **social justice**
- Expand **education** opportunities
- Support **arts and culture**

---

[9] *Ibid.*, p. 21.

- Provide **disaster relief**
- Increase **social welfare**

Whom will you help?

- **Age group**, e.g. children, youth adults, elderly
- **Gender**, e.g. women/girls
- **Populations**, e.g. rural, immigrant, ethnic, or religious community
- **Social economic communities**, e.g. the destitute, budding entrepreneurs, small business owners

Where will you act?

- At home or abroad?
- At what level? Global, regional country, community."

(*Source*: UBS Philanthropy Compass, Zurich 2014, 23.[10])

8.1.2 Self-assessment of One's Values and Resources

For a self-assessment of one's own values, the following table (Table 8.1) is useful. It can be used to get clarity for any kind of goals and decisions made by philanthropists as founders of foundations, as investors, as employees or as project implementers.[11]

8.2 Governance and Strategic Management

8.2.1 The Term "Governance"

Governance refers to "all the processes of governing, whether undertaken by a government, market, or network, whether over a family, tribe, formal or informal organization, or territory, and whether through laws, norms, power, or language. … It relates to *the processes of interaction and decision-making among the actors* involved in a collective problem that

---

[10]Free download: www.ubs.com/philanthropy.
[11]From Stückelberger (2014, pp. 54–56).

Table 8.1.   Self-assessment of one's own values, virtues, and resources.

My Values, Virtues, Resources	
My name:	
My institution and function in the institution:	
Values	**My answers**
Responsibility (response to power): What does it mean in my leadership role? What is its importance for me? How can I strengthen it?	
Justice/equity (in its various forms): What does it mean in my leadership role? What is its importance for me? How can I strengthen it?	
Solidarity (compassion and engagement): What does it mean in my leadership role? What is its importance for me? How can I strengthen it?	
Empowerment (enabling and strengthening personal competence): What does it mean in my leadership role? What is its importance for me? How can I strengthen it?	
Community/participation (recognizing the dignity of each human being and integrating their contribution): What does it mean in my leadership role? What is its importance for me? How can I strengthen it?	
Trust (relation despite uncertainty): What does it mean in my leadership role? What is its importance for me? How can I strengthen it?	
Transparency (openness/clarity and accountability): What does it mean in my leadership role? What is its importance for me? How can I strengthen it?	
Virtues	**My answers**
Integrity (honesty, openness, transparency): What does it mean in my leadership role? What is its importance for me? How can I strengthen it?	
Modesty (free from greed and arrogance): What does it mean in my leadership role? What is its importance for me? How can I strengthen it?	
Service (courage to serve the common good and common cause): What does it mean in my leadership role? What is its importance for me? How can I strengthen it?	
Forgiveness (being able to accept one's mistakes and forgive others): What does it mean in my leadership role? What is its importance for me? How can I strengthen it?	
Empathy (ability to empathize and care for others): What does it mean in my leadership role? What is its importance for me? How can I strengthen it?	

(Continued)

Table 8.1.   (*Continued*)

Faithfulness (faithful to values and promises): What does it mean in my leadership role? What is its importance for me? How can I strengthen it?

Carefulness (prudence in the management of resources and people): What does it mean in my leadership role? What is its importance for me? How can I strengthen it?

My Personal Resources   **My answers**

General: What are my various sources of energy and motivation? How can I attend to them?

My safety nets: What are my safety nets/ relations in times of crisis and need for orientation in leadership? How can I improve them?

My coach: Who is my personal coach, my pastor and "auditor" for my leadership?

My faith/spirituality: Is my faith/spirituality a source of energy and motivation? If yes, how? Which rituals? If not, why?

My material resources: How can they be used for my values, virtues? Which portion is for myself, my professional goals, my family, and my philanthropic engagement?

---

lead to the creation, reinforcement, or reproduction of social norms and institutions."[12]

Whatever "form" an entity may take, its "*governance* is the way the rules, norms and actions are produced, sustained, regulated and held accountable. The degree of formality depends on the internal rules of an given organization. … As such, governance may take many forms, driven by many different motivations and with many different results."[13] For instance, a non-profit organization, such as a public benefit foundation, may be governed by a small board of directors and pursue more specific aims.

A foundation has a dual focus: achieving the organization's social mission and ensuring the organization is viable. "Both responsibilities relate to fiduciary responsibility that a board of trustees (sometimes called directors, or Board, or Management Committee — the terms are

---

[12] Wikipedia. More in Swiss Foundation (2016, 2007).

[13] Wikipedia on Governance, *op. cit.*

interchangeable) has with respect to the exercise of authority over the explicit actions the organization takes. Public trust and accountability is an essential aspect of organizational viability so it achieves the social mission in a way that is respected by those whom the organization serves as well as the society in which it is located."[14]

When discussing governance in particular organizations, the quality of governance within the organization is often compared to a standard of good governance. In the case of a non-profit organization or a foundation, for example, "good governance relates to consistent management, cohesive policies, guidance, processes and decision-rights for a given area of responsibility, and proper oversight and accountability."[15]

The not-for-profit sector can profit a lot from good governance criteria and experiences in the public sector and the private business sector.[16] But foundations also have their specificities, which have to be considered.

8.2.2 Strategic Management

Up to now, you have formed your vision, mission, and values through asking yourself questions about what kind of philanthropist you want to be: what, whom, and where does your philanthropic activity or foundation want to focus on? What approach do you want to take? Now, developing a strategy, along with a set of management tools for fulfilling your mission and your goals, is the next step. "A *strategy* sets out what needs to happen for your goals to be reached, how those actions fit together, and where you will act."[17]

8.2.2.1 *Developing a strategy*

For developing your strategy, the following steps and points are practical considerations. Let us refer again to the very helpful, practical guide of the Union Bank of Switzerland (UBS) in its Philanthropy Compass[18]:

---

[14] *Ibid.*

[15] *Ibid.*

[16] E.g. Hilb (2016).

[17] UBS Philanthropy Compass, Zurich 2014, 32.

[18] *Ibid.*, 34f. Free download: www.ubs.com/philanthropy.

"Step 1: Select goals and objectives
- What is your hypothesis of what is the specific issue you are trying to solve (used to develop your approach)?
- Based on your vision, what are your objectives? What exactly is it that you want to achieve?
- What impact do you want to have on these priorities? Which specific goals do you want to achieve?"

"Step 2: Identify possible activities
- What will it take to solve the issues you have identified? What are the different ways that the issues could be addressed? What changes would need to take place?
- What are the available options to bring about these changes? What has worked well in the past?
- What resources are needed to carry out the necessary activities?
- Who else is working on this? Are there gaps that have not been addressed by other players?
- Are there opportunities for collaboration?"

"Step 3: Choose your course of action
- Which of the various options identified in Step 2 best fit your philanthropic approach?
- What can you be most helpful with, given your resources, networks, and expertise?
- What activities will you pursue?
- Whom should you collaborate with?
- How can you build on what others are doing?"

"Step 4: Map your logical model
There are many competing names for what is called the "logical model," for example, "logical framework" or "logical chain." The model includes a planning phase in which you set your goal and objectives and plan your activities. Those will be supported by the resources you can contribute. Thereafter in an evaluation phase you can look at your outputs (i.e. the results of your activities), the outcomes (which are your desired objectives), and the impact (your desired goal)."[19]

---

[19] *Ibid.*

8.2.2.2 *Organizational structure and human resources management*

Choosing the board and right staff are particularly important if you want your philanthropy or your foundation to continue beyond your lifetime; or if your personal involvement is limited. In the case that you have decided to set up a foundation, you will need to reflect on the governance and leadership structure: board and staff. In most jurisdictions, a board of directors is a legal requirement for a foundation. It has the final decision-making power and the responsibility and liability.

The *composition of the board*[20] should be coherent with the objectives of the foundation (e.g. expertise of board members), the geographical outreach and character of the foundation (e.g. only local members or an international Board), and most important the trust and relationship to the founder and the other members, to have enough unity, but also enough diversity (gender, age, background), which is also important for the reputation of the Board.

Concrete questions to ask for building a board and select staff[21]:

"(A) What is a board? Why is a board needed?
A board for a foundation is a voluntary body that has a legal duty to oversee how a foundation is run and is a key element of governance. A board's core functions can be summarized as:

- *mission oversight*: ensuring that the activities of the foundation contribute to its mission;
- *fiduciary oversight*: ensuring that endowments are invested well, and the operation is run efficiently.

A board may also get involved in implementing your foundation's vision (advice, advocacy, grant decisions, etc.). This depends on the nature of your philanthropy. In addition, you can have other bodies to provide advice such as an advisory board or a technical committee."

A diverse board (in terms of cultural background, gender, professional experience, relevant expertise) is a reservoir of ideas and innovation.

---

[20] Hilb (2016), *op. cit.*
[21] UBS Philanthropy Compass, Zurich 2014, p. 61f. Free download: www.ubs.com/philanthropy.

When setting up a board, one should pay attention to the following points:

- Setting a (renewable) fixed term for the board, e.g. 2, 3, or 5 year terms, renewable three times up to a maximum of eight years.
- Providing opportunity to periodically reassess its composition, and to make changes as necessary.
- Making sure to identify potential conflicts of interest (a declaration of potential conflicts of interest signed by all board and staff members annually becomes more and more a standard).[22]
- Determining the board's strategic role at the outset. Board members are most effective when given specific, defined roles that are adhered to. Agreeing on expectations ensures that tasks are efficiently executed.

(B) *Why might staff be needed?*
(Paid) employees are staff who manage and implement activities in order to realize the foundation's vision and goals. There are three basic types of staff:

- "Administrative staff handles day-to-day operations (e.g. processing grant applications, taking board minutes, or fulfilling legal reporting requirements).
- Programme staff helps implement your philanthropic vision (e.g. evaluating grantees, managing projects, researches, etc.)"[23]
- Interns and volunteers are important for social organizations. They are normally non-remunerated and get compensation only for expenses or allowances for food and shelter. This depends on legislation of the respective countries and the policies of the foundation.

(C) *Hire a manager you trust and connect with*
- "It is easy to underestimate how engaged in the foundation you will want to be, even if you take a more hands-off role. Therefore, working together with a manager that shares your vision, whom you trust and relate with well personally, is essential."[24] Depending on the legislation

---

[22] See as example the Declaration on Conflicts of Interest of Globethics.net Foundation: http://www.globethics.net/ethical-profile.
[23] UBS Philanthropy Compass (2014), *op. cit.*, p. 61.
[24] *Ibid.*, p. 64.

of the country, the founder, the chairperson, and the manager of the foundation is allowed to be the same person, but for reasons of good governance and control of power, the separation of the position of the president and the director among two persons is the normal case and creates more trust and transparency.

(D) *Compensate staff appropriately*
- It is natural to want to devote as much of your resources as you can to your philanthropy. However, to deliver effectively on your vision, the foundation will have to invest to attract well-qualified, high-calibre staff.

(E) *Consider outsourcing activities*
- It is not always necessary to hire a new employee just because a job or a new project needs to be implemented. If the role is time-limited or self-contained, it may be more efficient to bring in an external partner."[25]
- Outsource the task to a partner organization or work with volunteers who can be at the same time experts in the respective fields. Many retired specialists are offering their services and are looking for such opportunities. The Swiss development organization *Swisscontact*, specialized in technical development projects, every year engages over 100 retired technical experts as volunteers through their "Senior Expert Corps."[26]

To summarize, a board provides legally mandated oversight for a foundation. The right board and staff can extend your capacity to pursue your vision, and increase your effectiveness. In doing so, the right board members and staff can share the workload, responsibilities, reduce risk, and contribute to the impact and success of your philanthropic activities.

8.2.2.3 *SWOT — A Strategic Management Analysis Tool*

A *SWOT analysis*[27] is a planning method to evaluate the *Strengths, Weaknesses, Opportunities, and Threats (SWOT)* of a project or a business

---

[25] *Ibid.*

[26] *Swisscontact*: http://www.swisscontact.org/en/your-commitment/project-engagement/senior-expert-corps.html.

[27] See e.g. https://en.wikipedia.org/wiki/SWOT_analysis.

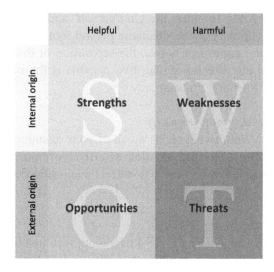

Figure 8.2.   SWOT analysis.

(see Figure 8.2). A SWOT analysis can be carried out for all kind of projects, activities, institutions, and planning processes. It is often used in strategic planning. It considers internal (strengths and weaknesses) and external (opportunities and threats) factors.

- *Strengths*: Characteristics of a project or institution that give an advantage over others.
- *Weaknesses*: Characteristics of a project or institutions that are a disadvantage compared to others.
- *Opportunities*: External factors in society, market, research, media, networks, etc. that could be used as an advantage.
- *Threats*: External factors and trends in society, market, research, media, networks, etc. that could endanger the project or institution.

"Identification of SWOT is important because they can inform later steps in planning to achieve the objective. First, the decision makers should consider whether the objective is attainable, given the SWOT. If the objective is *not* attainable, they must select a different objective and repeat the process."[28]

---

[28] *Ibid.*

Table 8.2.   A simple SWOT Analysis used in a foundation.

Strengths and Weaknesses	Opportunities and Threats
Internal factors	**External factors**
• Human resources	• Trends (new research)
• Financial resources	• Cultural, political, economic, and
• Organizational resources	religious environment
• Physical resources	• Funding sources
• Internal advantages/disadvantages	• Current events
of the Organization	• Freedom or oppression of
• Experiences	institutions in society
• Expertise	• Foundation legislation
• Networks	

The SWOT analysis can be used effectively to build an organization's or a personal strategy (see Table 8.2). Steps that are necessary to execute strategy-oriented analysis involve: identification of internal and external factors (using popular 2×2 matrix), selection and evaluation of the most important factors, and identification of relations existing between internal and external features.

For instance: strong relations between strengths and opportunities can suggest the good condition of an organization and allow using an *aggressive* strategy. Conversely, strong interaction between weaknesses and threats could be analysed as a potential warning and indicate using a *defensive* strategy.

"The SWOT analysis has been utilized in not-for-profit foundations as a tool to identify positive and negative factors within organizations, communities, and the broader society that promote or inhibit successful implementation of social services and social change 'efforts.'" This management tool is best used before developing goals and objectives for a programme or a project design or implementing an organizing strategy.

8.3 Action Plans: Project Development, Management, Accountability, and Evaluation

From the previous section, it has been seen that by selecting a vision and a strategy, a foundation or a philanthropist would have made important progress on narrowing down what he/she/it wants to do. There are still many decisions to be made in order to translate these approaches into actions.

8.3.1 Project Development

When working on development of *programmes*, while keeping the vision and the overall strategy framework in mind, you should be clear about which of the specific needs and opportunities within your area of interests you will address. And which strategy will you pursue to reach your goals. Keeping this overall line in mind, a foundation leader or philanthropist needs to identify and develop the programmes they wish to fund/run, assess them, and determine how they can find the right people and/or organizations/partners for managing and running those projects.

The term programme refers to a larger set of activities that is composed of different projects. A programme (as its *projects*) is a journey, not a destination; it is a path having a purpose and a limited period. It is therefore not obvious to define a project as a permanent activity. Today, each not-for-profit organization (NPO) must be innovative in its operation and be able to adapt to new needs, new challenges as well as new targets. Finding the right balance between stability, reliability, sustainability, and innovation is the real challenge for every NPO. Innovation and managing new projects involve the capability of asking the right questions, to meticulously prepare development of programmes, and the detailed planning of projects. The resources of an NPO are often uncertain, it is the responsibility of each manager to take care of, and not to endanger, these resources; in other words, seeking to manage a project at best thus ensuring the sustainability of the organization. Managing an NPO as a whole requires an excellent picture of all activities conducted in each project. To prevent the proliferation of projects, it is useful to develop criteria to guide the choice of any new projects. Setting goals for each project is fundamental. Objectives for each project should be identified as to be reachable with the relevant strategies and measures of an NPO. One must define, in the short, medium, and long term, what an organization intends to achieve through these projects. They must be expressed as concretely as possible so that one is able to assess the achievement of each project thereafter. The following questions need to be asked when selecting a project:

- What objectives does the project aim to achieve?
- What kind of needs does the project meet?
- What problems does the project seek to address?

8.3.2 SMART Tool in Project Management

When selecting a project and properly formulating the objectives of a project, it is always advisable to use the *SMART* tool and to respect what SMART really signifies as as acronym. The term stands for: *Specific, Measurable, Achievable, Realistic,* and *Time-Bound.* The formulation of a project should specifically integrate the following criteria:

- *Define the content*: What should be the goal = what?
- *Define the scope*: What is the level of the goal = how much?
- *Define the segment*: Which target group(s) should it reach out to = to whom?
- *Define the area*: To what geographic area the objective must be addressed = where?
- *Define the time period*: Until when the objective(s) should be achieved = when?

In sum, no matter in what field (cultural, social, humanitarian, sport, religious, etc.), any NPO engaged in any activity and project should always first ask the aforementioned questions before taking any commitments and actual actions. The action plans of programmes and projects should be formulated through asking these questions and defining their corresponding answers. Undertaking activities without really understanding goals, or establishing purposes of a project, is a waste of time and energy, and any faults due to not having realized the importance of defining goals of a project/activity are really strategic mistakes. Every action must have its usefulness. Donors today are more concerned than ever about the good use of their funds and about the capability of a project manager before they consider giving their financial commitment.

Once the projects are well defined as per the above process, then it is time for the next phase — of planning and execution. While planning, one needs to first set a framework, and to consider costs, revenues, risks, resources, methods, time, and other factors; then start to execute and to put the projects into action. One should also take into consideration the progress reporting and assessment of results in each phase while distributing results in each stage with the aim of ensuring each project being executed and in progress is as intended and as planned.

8.3.3 Accountability and Evaluation

We look at accountability for a foundation from two perspectives: (1) financial accountability (accounts and balance sheet); (2) accountability towards its donors/financial partners in terms of impacts, results, and achievements of the foundation.

8.3.3.1 *Financial Accountability*

Rigorous financial planning should enable any organizations to manage its daily operations at best, especially to avoid taking financial risks, which excessively jeopardize the organization as a whole. The strategy of an organization, and thought, should allow it to bring out the following:

- What goals it wants to achieve (objectives)?
- What it wants to do over the next few years (main activities, milestones)?
- For which target groups/beneficiaries (that is for whom the activity is intended)?
- Where, on which territory (where the activity will be deployed)?

Setting these first strategic lines allows a foundation to closely look at related costs and revenues, in other words — financial accountability. As a pilot, it is better to ask a number of fundamental questions before take-off: first, one needs to define budgets for the next period (1, 3, or 5 years); then one needs to have a good understanding of the interdependence between budget and accounting. A *budget* is a strategic tool to plan, coordinate, communicate, motivate, monitor, and evaluate. It is a tool of strategic decision-making for anyone in charge of a project; it enables the development of future assumptions. *Accounting* is itself a tool of synthesis and analysis based on the past. It allows to visualize and establish a photograph of the past year and to analyse past results. Accounting, is required to meet legal obligations. "Integrated Reporting"[29] as a new global reporting standard looks then not only at single figures but at the overall objectives, strategies, and impacts of the organization, on the beneficiaries, the society, the environment, and above all on the values.

In summary: budgets represent the future, while accounting is about the past. The forecast is the role of budgets. Measuring achievements is the role of accounting by the establishment of a balance sheet, an income statement, a monitoring of the treasury. It is necessary to be very careful never to do a "cut and paste" from year to year. To manage a foundation in a financially accountable manner, its leader needs to respect a strict process between budgeting and accounting so that the interdependence of the two tools can be expressed optimally. To do so, the *following key steps* must be followed, for regular gap analysis and establishment of comparison charts between budgeting and accounting.

(1) The reconciliation comparison between budget and accounting should not be done only at the end of the year (balance sheet) but at very regular basis throughout the year, e.g. quarterly.

(2) The "controlling" or comparing between revenues, and budgeted and realized expenditure, should be conducted at least quarterly, to observe the differences and/or overruns in a timely manner, thus to be able to respond effectively.

(3) Do not be afraid of profit. There is often a confusion in understanding the term "non-profit organization." Recall some basic principles: an entity type association, foundation, which would have generated during its financial year a surplus of income, may use this benefit as it sees fit. This is why it is more precise to call it "not-for-profit organisation" instead of "non-profit organisation." Profit cannot be redistributed to donors like dividends in a private company — that is a condition for being tax-exempt as a foundation — but profit can be re-assigned entirely inside the organization:

---

[29] See Integrated Reporting, *The Integrated Reporting Framework* (since 2022 part of The International Financial Reporting Standards Foundation IFRSF), https://www.integratedreporting.org. Globethics.net is a member of its International Integrated Reporting Council IIRC.

- for achieving the organization's mission;
- for developing and expanding programmes;
- for building up its reserves; and
- for investments to generate income from foundation assets.

The leadership of a foundation will be in no way receiving a bonus or premium based on financial results. Nevertheless, the organization may and should make a profit. This profit ideally should be used as a reserve, this will allow the organization to assume its financial responsibilities towards its beneficiaries when operations in a given year are more difficult than another (i.e. massive drop of donations, loss of a financial partner, etc.). In view of today's difficult and competitive environment that each organization must daily confront, it is considered by many donors that the creation of reserves has become a quasi-obligation for all NPOs if they want to survive. It is also suggested that a foundation should have a professional accountant to manage accounts while overseeing budgeting.

8.3.3.2 *Results, Impacts, and Evaluation*

Evaluation is a way of systematically gathering and reviewing information to assess the impacts of your programmes/projects. It also means asking smart, timely questions about your philanthropic/foundation's work to understand and increase your impact. Going through the *evaluation process*,

- "it allows you to understand more about the issues you seek to address
- it allows you to check whether your approach is having an impact
- it enables you to be more effective in how you act
- it helps you understand how to replicate and scale your successful initiatives
- it can demonstrate your credibility to other funders, government, society and donors
- it can provide supporting evidence for policy or advocacy work."[30]

---

[30] UBS Philanthropy Compass, Zurich 2014, 47. Free download: www.ubs.com/philanthropy.

Through the evaluation process, you can also learn what is working (and why), how you are progressing towards your goals, and whether the assumptions you made in your strategy are still true. When one says that a foundation can develop and learn from an evaluation, the following questions may be asked[31]:

"What type of questions should I ask?

- Are partners doing what they said they would do?
- Are things costing much more or much less than planned? Why?
- What does that mean for the work-plan?
- Are things going according to plan?
- Are you getting the results you hoped for?
- Why, or why not?
- How should you adapt or improve your way of working?
- Do the outcomes you are striving for seem to be having the desired effect?
- Are assumptions of your theory of change correct?
- How should you adapt or improve your strategy?"[32]

"Why do I need to know?

- To ensure that your resources are used efficiently, as you intended;
- To see whether things are unfolding as planned, and if you need to make changes to achieve your intended outcomes;
- To refine your strategy and theory of change, and to validate your work, so that others can build on it."[33]

"Where do I find the information (the means of verification)?

- Regular reports from partners/grantees;
- A simple, standardized process (e.g. quarterly report, regular phone call, etc.);
- Periodic questions to beneficiaries and/or other stakeholders;
- Some questions will need to be tailored to the specific initiative;
- Data collected via an evaluator — as internal or external evaluation;

---

[31] *Ibid.*, p. 49.
[32] *Ibid.*
[33] *Ibid.*

- to include information from partners/grantees, other stakeholders and third parties;
- where appropriate, a baseline/framework should be set at the start of an initiative."

"What do I do with the answers when I get them?"

- Guard against corruption;
- Demonstrate compliance with local laws;
- Ensure your money/other resources is/are being used wisely;
- Work with partners to improve implementation;
- Focus resources on the most impactful activities;
- Share process lessons;
- Refine your strategy and identify new opportunities;
- Demonstrate value to other donors and policymakers."[34]

Now through the evaluation, a foundation or a philanthropist will have known:

- if it/he/she is moving in the right direction;
- how to track progress; and
- how to measure the impacts/achievements.

Thus, one can say that through an evaluation process, a philanthropist or a foundation would be in a better position to meet his/her/its impacts/results expectation.

8.4 Funding and Fund-raising

8.4.1 Types of Foundations

Related to their *funding*, there are three main types of charity organisations in general and foundations specifically:

(1) *Giving Foundations* have a large foundation capital, e.g. (a) in the form of a legacy given as an endowment fund to the foundation,

---

[34] *Ibid.*

(b) as a mixture of such a foundation capital and additional yearly income from foundation activities such as business. Giving foundations use the annual net benefit of the capital and additional revenue for project support in their own organization or donated to other organizations. Their income heavily depends on the financial market and on business achievements. With the financial crises since 2008, many foundations suffered from decreasing net income and had to cut their donations and their own infrastructure. These foundations are either only little known in the public since they do not need to do public fund-raising and marketing, or — as many foundations in the last 10 years did — become known through their public invitation to submit funding support requests.

(2) *Receiving Foundations* have only a small foundation capital (the minimum amount is required by the law of the state where the foundation has its legal registration, e.g. in Switzerland CHF 50,000). A key part of their activities is fund-raising: collecting funds from various sources (see what follows) for annual expenses for projects and administration and to build reserves for a sustainable development. Their income depends on their fund-raising skills, motivations, and the economic situation in the donor areas and sectors. They are normally known in the public since they have to do public fund-raising.

(3) *Receiving and Giving Foundations* have their own resources, receive donations from third parties, and give donations to third parties. Many foundations combine these activities. It means that they do not implement all projects themselves, but are direct implementers of some and donors and facilitators of other projects.

8.4.2 Types of Income Sources

Fund-raising as a source for generating income is a key and complex activity of foundations. The principle is the same in not-for-profit activities as in the profit sector: The business of business is to generate income, to maintain and create jobs, and to create value for society. The difference is "only" that in the non-profit organizations, the net benefit (donations and other income) has to be distributed to and invested in beneficiaries and cannot be given back to the donors or owners as is the case in business, e.g. through dividends for shareholders.

The income sources by category of donors and donations differ substantially between the donors. The following main income sources can be distinguished (the list is not exhaustive):

(1) *Donations from Individuals*
    1.1 Small private donations from many individuals
    1.2 Large private donations from few individuals (High Net-Worth Individuals)
    1.3 Legacies from individuals
(2) *Donations from Institutions*
- 2.1 From state: communes, cities, governments, intergovernmental institutions
- 2.2 From private sector companies and their foundations
- 2.3 From private foundations and organizations
- 2.4 Legacies from institutions
(3) *Income from Sales*
- 3.1 From sales of products, services, licences, patents
(4) *Income from Reserves/Investments*
- 4.1 From investments of own capital
- 4.2 From benefit sharing of capital of third parties
(5) *Income from In-kind Contributions*
- 5.1 Volunteering: donating time
- 5.2 Expertise: sharing of knowledge
- 5.3 Goods and services: donating material, infrastructure, facilities

8.4.3 Types of Donations

(1) *General*: A general donation is given to the institution, which then allocates it to a programme or project according to the needs and budget lines.
(2) *Project-related (earmarked)*: such donations are given for a specific programme, project, campaign, or even for an individual (scholarship, individual child).

Earmarked donations are a strong trend since donors want to have better control, a relation to the project/country/person. Institutional donors need to justify the donation as coherent with their strategy and priorities. Conversely, receiving institutions need enough general donations in order to balance over-funding and under-funding of projects to reach the overall goals of the philanthropic activity. General donations depend also on the trust of donors and their long-term relationship with an institution: the relationship, the trust in the leadership, and a transparent and credible information policy are key for general contributions.

8.4.4 Types of Fund-Raising Methods

The fund-raising channels and methods are very broad. Only the main types are mentioned here.[35]

(1) *Public Campaigns*: Larger organizations present a large national or regional fund-raising campaign once a year, e.g. as fund-raising week, among the public at large with public adverts, media events, mailings in all households, phone campaigns with direct calls, etc. In many countries, public radio and television channels offer public campaigns, e.g. in an emergency after an earthquake, and channel the donations through their partner institutions.

(2) *Websites*: The donation button on the website of the foundation is a necessity, but it normally does not create substantial donations as donors often want more specific information first. Websites with fund-raising platforms for various organizations are known in some contexts, more in the Anglo-Saxon world than, e.g. in Europe.

(3) *Direct Mailings*: Emails and postal mailings addressed to the members of an organization or to selected addresses which are bought are a good, targeted way of fund-raising. Categories of addresses are distinguished: regular donors are "hot" addresses, random, rare donors are "warm" addresses, and bought addresses of persons who are not yet donors are called "cold" addresses. The "warmer" the address, the better the return of donations.

(4) *CrowdFunding*: Crowdfunding platforms allow individuals or institutions to fund-raise for a specific project, for a defined target amount, and during a limited time period. In emotionally touching projects like supporting a sick child, it can be very successful, in other cases, it is a failure. Transparency of reporting in private crowdfunding is often a challenge and does not always meet the

---

[35]See e.g. Taggert (2015), Keegan (2002), Chiukati (2009), Fundraising Akademie (2016).

standards of institutional fund-raising. But crowdfunding is also used by public media channels or social media with a list of projects, e.g. by Tencent in China, with great success of small amounts per donor but a very large number of donors (e.g. Tencent with an average of few dollars per donation but millions of young donors).

(5) *Direct Contacts*: Personal contacts by word-of-mouth marketing within families or neighbourhoods or even door-to-door collections are still an effective way of fund-raising, but need volunteers and some courage.

(6) *Collection at Events*: World over the most often used way of getting donations is still religious events, such as the collection in Christian Sunday worship, in the Muslim Friday prayer, and in the Hindu or Buddhist temple offerings. Other fund-raising events are benefit concerts, sport events, running (children get an amount per donor per km they run), etc.

(7) *Regular Transfer (Debit Procedures)*: Donors who are committed to an organization allocate regularly, e.g. once per month, an amount per automatic debit procedure from their bank account.

(8) *Applications to Institutions*: An important method is individual applications to institutions such as foundations, governmental agencies/state departments, companies and their foundations, multilateral institutions, etc. The applications are either proactive or as an answer to a call for applications by the respective institution.

(9) *Intermediaries, Especially Financial Institutions*: Banks and wealth managers influence the investment and also donation policies and decisions of their clients. A personal contact or a flyer in the hand of a wealth manager can motivate her/him to recommend a project or a foundation for a donation. Aged persons sometimes ask lawyers, pastors, and notaries to make suggestions for legacies to philanthropic institutions.

(10) *Directories*: Being listed in directories of foundations, and placing adverts in such directories, are mainly "branding marketing" in order to make an organization known.

(11) *Media Presence*: The presence of an organization in the media by way of interviews, reports about projects, advocacy, petitions, public controversies, and social media messages such as tweets and facebook groups is important to make an organization known and create the foundation for receiving donations.

(12) *Personalities*: Having a well-known personality such as a movie or sport star as president, board member, or director of an

Table 8.3. SWOT Analysis for the foundation's fund-raising strategy.

Strengths	Opportunities
• Resources and skills	• Innovative projects and approaches
• Relations, partnerships, networks	• Synergies with partner institutions
• Advantages compared to competitors	• Comparative advantage with new target
• Vision, values, reputation	groups
• Geographic location	• Expansion to new geographic areas, etc.
• Access to media, technologies, etc.	
Weaknesses	**Threats/Obstacles**
• Lack of history or success stories	• Changing laws in the donor countries
• Little transparency and accountability	• Political and economic unrest in the
• Geographic limitations	project countries
• Lack of significant networks, etc.	• Scandals in the organization or the
	non-profit sector of the country

organization, or as a special "ambassador," increases visibility and credibility of an organization as basis for donations.

8.4.5 The Fund-Raising Culture and Strategy

The income sources and the fund-raising methods depend on many factors such as the philanthropy culture in a geographic area, the social structure of society, fund-raising traditions, the religious background of donors, the legal framework and legislation for philanthropy activities, the tax deductibility, the technological facilities such as payment systems, social media, costs of adverts, and much more.

Fund-raising can learn from marketing strategies for consumer products. A philanthropic institution "markets" the projects similar to a product. Therefore, a foundation needs to make a market analysis of the fundraising market to find the most promising methods for fundraising, e.g. with a SWOT analysis (see Table 8.3).

8.5 Communication, Marketing, Reporting

8.5.1 Goals of Communication

Communication, marketing, and reporting are key activities for philanthropic institutions to:

- Raise funds since fund-raising is at the core a communication activity;
- Build trust by transparency;
- Report to donors about the use and impact of the donation;
- Meet legal reporting requirements of not-for-profit institutions;
- Build and sustain relationship with the beneficiaries of the programmes;
- Building bridges by increasing mutual understanding between donors, beneficiaries, and and intermediaries;
- Make the programmes and activities of the institution known to the larger public;
- Encourage others by sharing success stories.

8.5.2 Strategy of Communication

The strategy for communication, marketing, and reporting depends on the objectives and the culture of the organization. In the past, many private foundations — especially small foundations or those with endowment funds and no need for extended public fund-raising activities — cultivated a culture of confidentiality. Some of them have no website, no publicly available report, and are difficult to contact. They protect themselves also from being overwhelmed by numerous funding applications since they already know what they support and they may not be open or do not have additional funds for new applications.

This strategy is understandable and can be justified for the reasons given. In some exceptional cases, confidentiality is intended if money-laundering of money with corruption or black market background is involved. But with the international transparency standards in banking and financial transactions, not-for-profit institutions are closely monitored by the supervisory authorities and the financial institutions and are obliged to implement transparency standards.

The majority of not-for-profit institutions have remarkably increased the transparency and amount of information on their websites. They respond to the trend of donors who want to know more about the activities and want to monitor and have direct contacts with beneficiaries. In addition, new social media and crowdfunding facilitate this new trend.

We recommend that not-for-profit institutions follow a proactive, open communication strategy to build trust and transparency. The comparison of not-for-profit institutions by rating them becomes more and more popular. For example, the China Foundation Centre (CFC), a private rating agency for Chinese foundations, makes it a condition for foundations to be listed in their directory that they publish their annual report and annual account. This led to the fact that only recently (2016/2017), the number of Chinese foundations that published this information grew very substantially, as can be seen on the website of CFC.[36] CFC offers on its website the very informative "China Foundation Transparency Index" with a lot of information about 4,225 foundations (as of 20 March 2017).[37]

It does not mean that it can be justified to keep some information confidential. For example, if beneficiaries are endangered by the release of information of support in countries of war, terrorism, dictatorship, or threats against journalists up to murdering of journalists, one may need to be very cautious about which information is released and to whom. It is not unethical, but ethical to do so to protect lives.

---

[36] http://en.foundationcenter.org.cn/.
[37] http://ftien.foundationcenter.org.cn/.

Chapter 9

Conclusion and Outlook:
Innovation in Philanthropy

For the last two to three decades, China as well as all European countries have recognized the role of philanthropy, which benefits the public interest and helps to minimize social conflict. The tax incentive mechanisms, the legally favourable environment for foundations, increased awareness of the need for philanthropy and professionalism are factors that contribute to this megatrend.

Some countries have a longer philanthropic tradition compared to others. At the same time, behaviours in terms of individual giving are very disparate, given the wide variety of historic and cultural backgrounds, socio-economic factors, state models, and taxation rules. There is no one-size-fits-all portrait of the philanthropist or donor, nor are there dominant models. Nonetheless, in Europe especially the foundation sector is flourishing since many philanthropists consider constituting a foundation as one of the best instruments in pursuing their philanthropic vision and wishes and having full control over it. But this trend is also a weakness because many foundations are extremely small, without staff, and have low impact if they are not linked to larger and experienced institutions with similar objectives.

Traditional philanthropy is most commonly associated with straightforward grantmaking, most usually making donations where all capital is lost and no return expected. The current practice of philanthropy is more sophisticated and diverse, and more and more foundations are not only or mainly grantmaking, but also implementing projects themselves. Today's European foundations are largely characterized by their youth and dynamism, a sign that the modern philanthropic culture is developing and lively. Adaptation of the legal and fiscal frameworks facilitates this trend. Foundations actively mobilize resources other than the initial endowments of legacies. Young and active European foundations define themselves primarily in terms of their actions rather than their assets. Through use of external resources, whether public or private, and not relying solely on the wealth of a single individual or family, the European foundations are mobilizing an increasing number of stakeholders, thus contributing to the wider deployment of a philanthropic culture.

Philanthropy is not a monopoly of European or American cultures, nor a 21st century phenomenon. *Chinese philanthropy* being largely formed by its traditional philosophy and culture, and much localized in kinship relationships, there is a renaissance of philanthropy in modern China. The modern philanthropy in China is a confluence of several complex factors, i.e. religious, historical, cultural, and political, as well as socio-reforms dimensions that shape expressions of philanthropic activities in China; it is highly likely that such profound factors will continue to influence the patterns and directions of modern Chinese philanthropy. Over the last two decades, a vital role for modern Chinese philanthropy has emerged in addressing the tension between wealth creation, poverty, and pressure on the environment. It is reasonable to assume that as more citizens in China grow wealthy, philanthropy will become an increasingly large component of spending — a phenomenon that is evolving and has been widely publicized in the current Chinese media.

Philanthropy is deeply rooted in all world religions: It was developed over thousands of years, and is especially strong in the Christian tradition. It had been deeply rooted in the Chinese traditional culture and had been practised by the Confucian merchants beginning in ancient Chinese history. Over the last 20 years, Western philanthropy has been through an accelerated period of change and evolution. Old money is being replaced by the new wealth of self-made entrepreneurs who want to be actively involved in their giving. Philanthropy has become a business sector like any other, focused on impact and outcomes; there are new financial tools and a paradigm shift from donating to investing through innovative entrepreneurial models of philanthropy. We live in a highly globalized world; learning from best practices globally and adapting to local needs and cultural contexts, the modern Chinese philanthropists are not just increasing the volume of giving by their wealthy, but are making their giving smart while becoming global citizens. In our view, philanthropy doesn't just have the latitude to innovate, it has a duty to do so, in order to adapt to the evolving needs in society and find the most efficient ways to deliver social impact. This view is also shared by the modern philanthropists all over the world. They are increasingly committing themselves to addressing social and environmental challenges through innovative philanthropic models, thus making philanthropy an industry and a major force for public good.

Innovation: This has led to wider deployment of philanthropic culture through entrepreneurial philanthropy, social responsibility, social impact, social innovation, social enterprises, etc. as these concepts have been applied in the philanthropy sector. Both Europe and China are seeing increased interest in *innovation in philanthropy*, in which *venture philanthropy, impact investing,* and *social entrepreneurship* are often used as instruments that bring financial investment strategies into line with the foundation's social mission. Although the social impact of these investment strategies is difficult to measure accurately at this point, it gives philanthropy a considerable pool of assets that can be mobilized to intensify the work of foundations to further the social good, while at the same time, decreasing their dependence on traditional donations and achieving financial sustainability.

With respect to supporting social entrepreneurship, traditional corporate charity has been shifting to the donation forms such as donating intelligence, platforms, technologies, and venture investment.

Nonetheless, we observe that the biggest challenges in the philanthropy industry are as follows:

- how to convert more entrepreneurs into social entrepreneurs so we can operate and manage non-profit organizations with more entrepreneurship, thus achieving a high degree of impact investing;
- how to attract more talent from different sectors into the philanthropic sector, to help expand the scale and impact of civil engagement and social responsibility.

In any case, we foresee that the philanthropy sector in both Europe and China, as in other world regions such as Asia outside China, Africa, and Latin America, has great space and opportunities to grow. But also the challenges are fast growing with dangerous and deep inequalities, environmental challenges, cultural, ethnic, and religious conflicts, racism, etc. May this book encourage all of us to be active in philanthropy and to do it in a professional way — doing good and doing it well.

Glossary

Definition of "Philanthropy"

The term *philanthropy* is generally used to describe any private voluntary action for the public good. It can encompass donations and investments of time, money, expertise, connections, and many other types of contribution of assets.[1] In this handbook, *philanthropy* is defined as any type of not-for-profit engagement by both individual donors and grantmaking foundations.

Charity, Philanthropy, and Diakonia

Charity

Charity, Latin *caritas*, means benevolence. It is a key term in Christian faith and theology. In the New Testament, the two-part commandment is the most famous core of charity: "Love God" and "Love your neighbour as yourself" (Mark 12:31). It is in fact a three-part commandment with the balance of the triangle of God, the other, and oneself. Charity is a value for society and a virtue[2] for personal behaviour. Thomas Aquinas understood it as "the friendship of man for God," which "unites us to God," and as "the most excellent of the virtues" (*ibid.*). Further, Aquinas holds that

---

[1] *Advancing Philanthropy in Switzerland: A Vision for a Cooperative and Recognized Philanthropic Sector*, published by Lombard Odier Darier Hentsch, Geneva, June 2010.
[2] See https://en.wikipedia.org/wiki/Charity_(virtue).

"the habit of charity extends not only to the love of God, but also to the love of our neighbour." Charity is based on Gods' love (Greek word agape, Αγάπη), meaning an unconditional love for others.

There are multiple meanings of the word "love" in modern languages: sexual love, emotional love, friendship, etc. In the Greek New Testament, there are different words for these dimensions: *Eros* as erotic and sexual love, *philia* as friendship, and *agape* as caring, benevolence, holistic support of the other up to the unity with the other as well as the profound acceptance of oneself. This love as *caritas* is divine energy residing in the *will* rather than emotions or sympathy, regardless of what emotions it stirs up. Thus, from Christianity's point of view, *charity* has two parts: love of God and love of people, which includes both love of one's neighbour and oneself. "Charity" is part of the Christian triple "faith, hope, and charity."[3]

Charity, compared to philanthropy, is today understood as emotion-driven giving and sharing with the needy (see Figure 1). This is a more superficial understanding than the original meaning of the word.

Figure 1.   Illustration of charity.

---

[3] Illustrations Left: Needham, Geo C., *Street Arabs and Gutter Snipes, 1884*. Right: Good Samaritan, Erlöserkirche Stuttgart. Artist Ulrich Hernn, Photo Ch. Stückelberger.

Philanthropy

Philanthropy (from Greek φιλανθρωπία) is etymologically composed of "philos"/"philia" (φίλος, friend/friendship) and "anthropos" (ἄνθρωπος, "human being"). "Philanthropist" can be translated as "friend of humans," "philanthropy" as "love of humans" or "love of humanity" in the sense of caring, nourishing, developing, and enhancing "what it is to be human" on both the side of the benefactors (by identifying and exercising their values in giving and volunteering) and beneficiaries (by benefiting). The most conventional modern definition is "private initiatives, for public good, focusing on quality of life." This combines the social scientific aspect developed in the 20th century with the original humanistic tradition, and serves to contrast philanthropy with business (private initiatives for private good, focusing on material prosperity) and *government* (public initiatives for public good, focusing on law and order).[4]

Diakonia

Diakonia — from the Greek word diakonein (to serve) — is the Christian term for service to others. The focus is on the needy in a community and in society in general. "Diakonia as Christian Social Practice"[5] includes all practical activities for the improvement of lives. It encompasses individual charity as well as large programmes for social justice.

Services in health, education, and poverty reduction have been the classical fields of Diakonia since the first years of Christianity. Throughout the past 2,000 years, education and health services have been to a large extent promoted and delivered by churches and Christian organizations. Diakonia is no more just "acting for" in terms of supporting the weaker, but means "working with" and empowering[6] the weak to take their life into their own hands and become independent from charitable support (empowerment approach). Diakonia is also engaged in peace-keeping and reconciliation[7] in order to eradicate the root causes of violence, terrorism, and war. Diakonia became also a Christian term for

---

[4] *Wikipedia* on "Philanthropy."
[5] Dietrich *et al.* (2014).
[6] Stanard and Emilio (2015).
[7] Lutheran World Federation (2009).

development work.[8] An example is the large German protestant development organization Bread for the World, which is part of the institution called "Evangelisches Werk für Diakonie und Entwicklung" (Protestant Service for Diakonia and Development), which includes Diakonia inside the country, international development work, international disaster relief, and interchurch help and advocacy. All this means that advocacy for structural change, rights of the weaker (rights-based approach), legislation (e.g. for a social security system in a social welfare state), and international conventions (e.g. for rights of children, right to food and water) became integral part of the modern understanding of Diakonia. Since two decades, the term Diakonia has enlarged in scope from human to non-human beings while speaking of "Diakonia for all creatures."[9]

The deacon (diakonos) — literally, "the servant" — became the term for the professional social workers in the church. In some countries, Christian social services are very limited by regulations or lack of financial and institutional means. In other countries, Christian diaconal institutions are among the largest in the modern social welfare state. In Germany, the churches with their diaconal institutions such as hospitals, kindergartens, schools, clinics, youth, and retirement programmes, etc. are the second largest employers with 1.3 million employees, after the state as the largest employer![10]

In view of the above, although there are different definitions of the three terms, in this handbook, we propose that:

(1) *Charity* means rather a one-off gift or action to solve somebody's or a group of people's immediate needs.
(2) *Philanthropy* is considered to be more of an approach or philosophy on how to make the world a better place to live in and how to improve the living circumstances of all the less privileged over a longer period of time.
(3) *Diakonia* means a holistic approach to services for and with the needy for their empowerment, peace, and sustainable development.

---

[8]Mtata (2013).

[9]For a historical overview in Switzerland, see Stückelberger (2016b, pp. 138–158).

[10]https://arbeits-abc.de/arbeitgeber-kirche-13-millionen-mitarbeiter-im-zeichen-des-kreuzes/.

In historical and geographical comparison, the terms philanthropy, charity, and diakonia show the modification of meanings over time and in content[11]: Whereas *charity* was a very positive word of benevolence and love for centuries, it has a rather negative connotation of paternalism and individualistic giving and is today less used than philanthropy, but still used wordwide. *Philanthropy, conversely,* was rarely used, but became a common term of the private "aid-industry" in the last decade and was mainly used in USA, India, and in the last decade also Europe. Diakonia is a very old term for Christian "charity," used over 2,000 years, but today it is rarely used and mainly in Central and Northern Europe, USA, Russia, and in churches.

Values

The different terms show that values (benchmarks) and virtues (individual behaviour) are presupposed in all three terms and concepts, but to some extent are also different or with different priorities.

Values (non-exhaustive list)	Virtues (non-exhaustive list)
• Benevolence	• Honesty
• Love	• Compassion
• Caring	• Transparency
• Fairness	• Accountability
• Justice	• Integrity
• Empowerment	• Empathy
• Sustainability	• Respect
• Peace/reconciliation	• Responsibility

Values and virtues influence the structure, goals, and praxis of a philanthropic entity and activity to a great extent. They:

- define what success for a philanthropic work looks like;
- signal to others what the philanthropic act is trying to achieve; and
- help to focus philanthropic activities on what is most important.

---

[11] Interesting developments can be seen based on google trends. Comparison of terms over time and regions can be searched. The limitation is that it is based on big data analysis of only online use of the terms. See on these three terms https://trends.google.com/trends/explore?date=all&q=philanthropy,charity,diakonia.

Foundations

The Term "Foundation"

A foundation is a non-profit legal entity. The legal forms are regulated by national or provincial laws and differ by country and tradition. In most jurisdictions, foundations require stronger criteria in terms of governance, transparency, and State control than non-profit associations or for-profit companies or cooperatives. Foundations in most countries are tax-exempt as they serve the common good and society and are not for profit of the owners or donors of the foundation. Foundations have no shareholders like companies and normally no members like an association, but they need to have a governing body, normally called a Board. This board can be very small with a minimum of three persons (e.g. comprising the Founder and family members) or very large when it comes to global foundations or semi-public foundations (foundations established by a State unit such as a ministry of the government).[12]

This type of foundation serving private purposes is typically endowed by an individual or family (see Figure 2). According to the European Foundation Centre (EFC), "private benefit foundations are those that pursue private

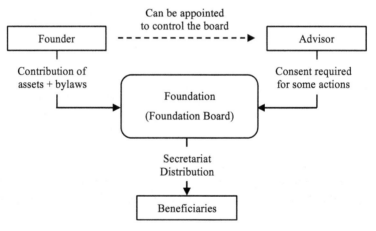

Figure 2.   A typical family foundation.

Note: "Family Foundations."

---

[12] *Ibid.*

purposes, such as the advancement of one family, relatives of the founder, trust funds for the education of the founder's children, etc." It is in this context that the terms "public benefit foundation" and "private benefit foundation" have come into practice.

There are three main types of foundations: (1) Grantmaking foundations, (2) Grantseeking foundations, and (3) A combination of both.[13] More information about this can be found in Chapter 8. Foundations as not-for-profit organizations are not allowed to pay back to founders or donors what was given as donation. This became very strict, especially to avoid any form of money laundering through tax-free foundations.

The Term "Public Benefit Foundation"

A generally accepted definition for the term "Public-benefit Foundation" is *private, independent organizations who work for the public good, and whose activities are intended to benefit the public.*[14] The "public-benefit foundations" are asset-based and purpose-driven.

In this handbook, we take the definition of EFC for the term "public-benefit foundation," which is widely accepted by the foundations sector in Europe. Based on the articles of the EFC's "Model Law for Public-Benefit Foundations in Europe" which were identified and agreed upon by experts and actors in the field among the EFC memberships, and *Comparative Highlights of Foundation Laws: The Operating Environment for Foundations in Europe* published by EFC in 2015, we propose that foundations are to be considered as "public-benefit foundations" if they meet the following five criteria:

(1) They are independent, separately constituted non-profit bodies.
(2) They have no shareholders.
(3) They have their own established and reliable source of income, usually but not exclusively from an endowment.
(4) They have their own governing board.
(5) They distribute their financial resources for educational, cultural, religious, social, or other public-benefit purposes, either by

---

[13] McGill (2015, p. 1).
[14] *Ibid.*, p. 3; also on EFC website.

- supporting associations, charities, and educational institutions or individuals; or
- operating their own programmes.[15]

During the past decades, almost all countries required foundations to possess a minimum level of assets as a condition of establishment (e.g. in Switzerland CHF 50,000 Foundation capital). Traditionally, many countries have also required foundations to hold additional capital to ensure that they have sufficient funds to pursue their stated purpose. In some cases, this takes the form of an *endowment* that is large enough to allow the foundation to operate its charitable programmes with support drawn largely (or entirely) from the interest income generated each year by the endowment.

According to the report *Comparative Foundation Laws in Europe*[16] "New forms of foundations, with new forms of income generation, have developed and it is becoming more important for the foundation to have *reliable mechanisms* in place to ensure that it has adequate financial resources to pursue its public-benefit purposes rather than to have a fixed amount of static capital at the moment of establishment."[17] On the fundraising implications, see Chapter 8.

It has become a trend that philanthropists set up their own foundations instead of donating to existing philanthropic institutions such as development organisations, youth, cancer, health, cultural, or research institutions. The advantage is full control and ownership, but it includes also higher risks of failures since philanthropy as a fruit of family business also needs family business governance.[18] Often, it is more efficient and professional to find an existing foundation or organization, which is able to assist in realizing their particular philanthropic wishes. The reason for this is simple: setting up a long-term philanthropic project, such as an agricultural development project in Africa, a green energy project in China, or an educational project in India's isolated poor regions, requires a different set of expertise that involves issues such as setting philanthropic objectives, formulating a giving strategy, presentation of strategy initiatives, technical advice, and projects and operational management. Family offices

---

[15] Please also refer McGill (2015), *op. cit.*, p. 3.

[16] European Foundation Sector Report 2015.

[17] McGill (2015), *op. cit.*, pp. 3–4. See also www.swissfoundations.ch.

[18] See the helpful handbook of the International Finance Corporation (2008).

share their experience in supporting donors in managing their wealth: "Even a smaller philanthropic project could prove quite difficult to manage once it has been set up. It would therefore be very useful if this handbook can support a practitioner in managing and monitoring the projects or help a philanthropist in formulating his or her philanthropic project. As you might well imagine, setting up a more sizeable, new philanthropic institution, to which external parties may also donate in the future, is a challenge that certainly needs knowledge in this sector, which is often referred to as the third sector apart from the private and public sectors."[19]

---

[19] Family Office Services Switzerland, *op. cit.*

References

Avantage Ventures (2011). *Beyond the Margin*. Pais: Avantage Ventures. www. avantageventures.com.

Bar, A. *et al.* (2012). Single Family offices in Switzerland. *PLC Multi-Jurisdictional Guides*, 13, 45.

Bastos de Morais, J.-C. and Stückelberger, Christoph. (2014). *Innovation Ethics. African and Global Perspectives*, Globethcis.net, Global Series No. 7. Geneva: Globethics.net. http://www.globethics.net/global-series.

Buckland, L., Hehenberger, L. *et al.* (2013, Summer). The growth of european venture philanthropy. *Stanford Social Innovation Review*, 33–39.

Chiukati, J. (2009). *Fundraising on the Internet*. Nairobi: Repared.

Clark, C., Emerson, J. *et al.* (2012). *Investing for Impact*. Zurich: Credit Suisse Research Institute.

CSR Asia & Embassy of Sweden (2015). *A Study on Corporate Social Responsibility Development and Trends in China*. Beijing.

Dietrich, S., Jorgensen, K., Karsrud Korslien, K., and Nordstokke, K. (Eds.). (2014). *Diakonia as Christian Social Practice. An Introduction*. Oxford: Oxford Center for Mission Studies.

Dubach, B. and Elisa, S. (2007). *Der Leitfaden für Gesuchsteller*. Frauenfeld: Huber.

Eckhardt, B., Jakob, D., and von Schnurbein, G. (2015). *Rapport sur les fondations en suisse 2015*, Vol. 14. Basel: CEPS-SwissFoundations.

Family Office Services Switzerland (FOSS), *Family Foundations*, without year. http://www.switzerland-family-office.com/foundation.html.

Fondation de France (2015). *A Flourishing European Philanthropy Sector*. Paris: Fondation de France.

Fulda, A. (2017). A new law in China is threatening the work of international NGOs. *The Conversation*, 6 January 2017. http://theconversation.com/a-new-law-in-china-is-threatening-the-work-of-international-ngos-70884.

Fundraising Akademie (Ed.). (2016). *Fundraising. Handbuch für Grundlagen, Strategien, Methoden*. Berlin: Springer Gabler.

Globethics.net. *Declaration on Conflicts of Interest of Globethics.net Foundation*: Free download: http://www.globethics.net/ethical-profile.

Ham Stanard, C. E. (2015). *Empowering Diakonia: A Model for Service and Transformation in the Ecumenical Movement and Local Congregations*. Amsterdam: Free University.

Hilb, M. (2016). *New Corporate Governance. Successful Board Management Tools* (5th edn.). Berlin: Springer.

Integrated Reporting. *The Integrated Reporting Framework* (since 2022 part of The International Financial Reporting Standards Foundation IFRSF). https://www.integratedreporting.org/.

International Finance Corporation (2008). *IFC Family Business Governance Handbook*. Washington: IFC.

Lai, W. (1992). Chinese Buddhist and Christian Charities: A comparative history. *Buddhist-Christian Studies*, 12.

Li, F. (2013). *Time for a Philanthropy Revolution in China*. Global Link Initiative, Skoll World Forum, 9 December 2013.

Li, J. and Stückelberger, C. (2017). *Philanthropy and Foundation Management. A Guide to Philanthropy in Europe and China*. Geneva: Globethics.net.

Liu, M. (China Representative, United Nations Global Compact) (17 March 2015). Is corporate social responsibility China's secret weapon? https://www.weforum.org/agenda/2015/03.

Lombard Odier Darier Hentsch (2010). *Report: Advancing Philanthropy in Switzerland — A Vision for a Cooperative and Recognized Philanthropic Sector*. Geneva: LODH/Fondation, 1796.

Lutheran World Federation (2009). *Diakonia in Context. Transformation, Reconciliation, Empowerment*. Geneva: LWF.

Mark 12:31. Holy Bible, New International Version®, NIV®. Copyright© 1973, 1978, 1984, 2011 by Biblica, Inc.®

McGill, L. T. (2015). *Number of Registered Public Benefit Foundations in Europe Exceeds 141,000*. Brussels: EFC.

Ministry of Civil Affairs of China (1998). *Regulations on the Registration and Administration of Social Organizations*. Beijing: MCAC.

Ministry of Civil Affairs of China (2004). *Regulations on the Administration of Foundations*. Beijing: MCAC.

Mtata, K. (Ed.) (2013). *Religion: Help or Hindrance to Development?* Leibzig: Lutheran World Federation/EVA.

O'Donohoe, L. *et al.* (2010). Impact investments: An emerging asset class. *J.P. Morgan Global Research.* www.morganmarkets.com.

Observatoire de la Fondation de France & CerPhi (2015). *An Overview of Philanthropy in Europe.* Paris: OF.

Porter, M. and Kramer, M. (2016). Philanthropy's new agenda: Creating value. *Harvard Business Review,* 77(6): 121–130.

Rob, J., Tan, P. *et al.* (2013). *Innovation in Asian Philanthropy: Entrepreneurial Social Finance in Asia.* Singapore: Asia Centre for Social Entrepreneurship and Philanthropy, National University of Singapore.

Russell, C. and Milo, Z. (2015). *The State of Philanthropy in China.* Beijing: CKGSB Knowledge.

Stückelberger, C. (2014). *Responsible Leadership Handbook. For Staff and Boards.* Globethics.net Praxis Series No. 1. Geneva: Globethics.net. http://www.globethics.net/praxis-series.

Stückelberger, C. (2016a). *Global Ethics Applied,* 4 volumes. Globethics.net Readers Series No. 1–4, Geneva: Globethics.net. http://www.globethics.net/readers-series.

Stückelberger, C. (2016b). *Sozialethik and Diakonie. Ethische, ekklesiologische und ökonomische Herausforderungen der diakonischen Arbeit in der Schweiz.* In C. Stückelberger, *Global Ethics Applied,* Vol. 3. Geneva: Globethics.net, pp. 138–158.

Stückelberger, C., Cui, W. *et al.* (2016). *Entrepreneurs with Christian Values. Training Handbook for 12 Modules,* Globethics.net China Christian Series No. 3. Geneva: Globethics.net. free download: http://www.globethics.net/china-christian-series.

Stückelberger, C., Fust, W., and Ike, O. (2016). *Global Ethics for Leadership. Values and Virtues for Life,* Globethics.net Global Series No. 13. Geneva: Globethics.net. http://www.globethics.net/global-series.

SwissFoundations (2016). *Swiss Foundation Code 2015. Principles and Recommendations for the Establishment and Management of Grant-making Foundations.* Basel: Helbing Lichtenhahn. www.swissfoundationcode.ch.

SwissFoundations (2007). *Professionelles Management von Stiftungen. Ein Leitfaden für Stiftungspraktiker.* Basel: Helbing Lichtenhahn.

Syntao. *CSR Reports of Chinese Companies.* Collected in an online collection. http://www.globethics.net/library/collections/chinese-csr-reports.

Taggert, A. (2015). *Fundraising. Crash Course!* (Kindle online).

Tang, C. (2001). *The First Hundred Years of Protestant Mission in China.* Hong Kong: Taosheng Publishing House.

The Christian Philanthropy Enterprise in Canton from the Last Qing Dynasty to the Republic China (1900–1949). Master Thesis. 2005. www.globethics.net, library.

Ting, K. H. (2000). *Love Never Ends*. Nanjing: Amity Printing.

VZ Vermögenszentrum & VZ Ratgeber Spenden und Stiften (2008). *Alles Wichtige zu Spenden, Vermächtnissen und Stiftungen. Mit Tipps zur Nachlassplanung und zum Steuern sparen*. Zürich: VZ Vermögenszentrum.

Wang, A. (2009). *Church in China: Faith, Ethics, Structure. The Heritage of the Reformation for the Future of the Church in China*. Bern: Peter Lang, pp. 479–484. www.globethics.net, library.

Wehner, T. (2009). *Corporate Citizenship Survey*. Zurich: Federal Technical University (ETH).

Weiss, T. and Clark, H. (2006). 'Venture philanthropy' is new buzz in business: Buffett, Gates not the only tycoons reshaping world of charitable giving. *NBC News* (Source: *Forbes*), 26 June 2006.

Zi, Z. J. (2015). *The Responsibility of Wealth and Evolution of Capitalism. Revelation of a Century's Development of American Philanthropy* (Book in Chinese). Shanghai: Shanghai Joint Publishing.

Chinese Language Sources

'2014 家族企业传承主题论坛: 话传承心得, 谋长青之道', 2014 Family Business Inheritance Theme Forum: Discussing inheritance experience and ways to achieve longevity. http://he.ce.cn/gd/201412/01.

'环球一周民意调查话题榜', 《环球时报》, 2014 年 11 月 28 日

《老子》七十七章

《孟子·公孙丑上》

人民网 - 人民日报, 《中华人民共和国慈善法》, 2016 年 3 月 20 日

《太上感应篇》

王淑琴 (2016),《中国经济伦理研究, 第二集》, 全球伦理网中国伦理系列 5.

张冬栎(总编译) (2011),《理解混合型融资战略为社会企业带来的真正潜力》, Impact Economy 论文 卷 2 (日内瓦: Maximilian Martin).

Sigrist, Ch, Heinz Rüegger (2017). 基督教服务事工导论 — 帮助事工的神学基础. *Diaconia: An Introduction. Theological Foundation of Christian Service*, Geneva: Globethics.net (also published in Nanjing/China).

Index

Printed in the United States
by Baker & Taylor Publisher Services